WARD PARKWAY

Early Plan

A CITY WITHIN A PARK

*One Hundred Years
of Parks and Boulevards
in Kansas City, Missouri*

A CITY WITHIN A PARK

❧

One Hundred Years
of Parks and Boulevards
in Kansas City, Missouri

by
Jane Mobley
and
Nancy Whitnell Harris

Published by The American Society of Landscape Architects
and
The Kansas City, Missouri Board of Parks & Recreation Commissioners.

Book design by Vivian L. Strand

*Printed in the United States of America
The Lowell Press, Kansas City, Missouri*

ISBN 0-932845-52-5

On the cover: Strolling in Swope Park, 1912.

This book
— like the parks and boulevards system it celebrates —
is for everyone who turns to nature for recreation
and restoration of body and spirit.

The exciting play of water over rock formations is a part of Kansas City's natural beauty and has been incorporated in this waterfall on Cliff Drive in Kessler Park (formerly North Terrace Park). The site of a drinking fountain in the park's original plan, the waterfall, dedicated in the fall of 1979, was redesigned by Larkin Associates to highlight the native limestone walls and the dramatic bluffs along the drive.

CONTENTS

The classical elegance of the Music Pavilion in Swope Park is a reminder of the combination of designed and natural beauty that was the basis of the City Beautiful ideal.

PREFACE

here are those now, and there were others in earlier times, who have declared without reservation that the park and boulevard system is Kansas City's most distinctive, and distinguished, feature. It is the one thing that gives this city a special stamp, separating it from other communities in America and abroad.

It would take a brave person, indeed, or a very foolish one to argue that New York's Central Park is anything short of an urban jewel, perhaps without parallel anywhere on earth.

Or that the view looking west from the Tuileries Garden in the center of Paris, across the vast Place de la Concorde and up the tree-lined Champs Elysees to the Arc de Triomphe is anything less than a triumph.

Many cities, perhaps most cities, have a feature or two which justifiably command admiration, even awe. What Kansas City has accomplished is something quite different. It is the cumulative impact of a century of achievement that wins acclaim.

It all began in earnest with George Kessler's plan of 1893. Looking at it almost 100 years later, it seems modest in scope. Just a handful of parks, a few of them connected by boulevards.

Then if you turn to a map of the system in 1991, it is easy to see the same philosophy has been carried forward to this day.

By now Kansas City has dozens of parks and playgrounds, many of them linked, as in Kessler's plan, by mile after mile of tree-lined boulevards. And here and there along the way is a fountain, a monument or a piece of sculpture.

Kessler insisted the rugged natural beauty of the land be preserved wherever possible. He felt much as Washington Irving did when he visited the Great Bend of the Missouri in the 1830s. Irving wrote that "the luxuriance and the beauty of the forests exceeded any that I have seen," adding that the site "wanted only a castle or a gentleman's seat, here and there interspersed, to have equaled the most celebrated park scenery in England."

It has been noted that Kessler's aim was not to dazzle, but to make this a more livable city. But what has been created does dazzle.

In 1946, the famed French writer, Andre Maurois, wrote: "Who in Europe, or in America for that matter, knows that Kansas City is one of the loveliest cities on earth? Yet it is true."

None of this came about by accident. Nor has it been a string of unending victories, one crowning the other. Instead, it has been a tough, uphill task from the start. There have been peaks, to be sure. There have also been chasms, some so grim the future seemed all but hopeless.

The challenges have come on many fronts and with varying degrees of severity. The periodic shortage of funds at City Hall when parks were treated as frills. The multiple plans to carve up the parks, to overdevelop them or to pave them over as if a few acres of grass and trees were somehow offensive to the eye. And then the greatest culprit of all, the elm bark beetle which devastated tens of thousands of trees, many of them in the parks and along the boulevards.

The plan to create the "City Beautiful" had a beginning, but happily no ending. Certainly it did not end with the boundaries of the city that were in place at the conclusion of the Second World War.

As Kansas City leaped the Missouri River, expanding far to the north, and at other times pushing to the south and the east, the park and boulevard system expanded, too. Not so fast as many would have liked, but the system did grow and it is still growing.

By 1975, two of the largest parks, Tiffany Springs near KCI and Jerry Smith Park, which is not far from Richards-Gebaur, were miles beyond the old city limits.

Over the last century many gifted people have played a crucial role in this remarkable saga. Some of them never backed off, no matter how tough the going or how slim the odds. And that has been true from the earliest dreamers, such as Kessler and August Meyer, right down to our own time when Anita Gorman and Frank Vaydik, among others, labored so diligently to preserve and expand what is essentially the same dream.

The following pages offer a lively, often dramatic, account of what has happened over the last century — and why.

— *Al Bohling*

INTRODUCTION

Y ou really have to like Kansas City. There is a sense about the place, that it is still a sort of picture book American Town; the kind of easy-to-read, open place where you can "lead the good life" today and, at the same time, have a belief in tomorrow. You get the impression that not only is everything "up to date," but that also the city is working away pretty effectively on whatever's before it. The intractable problems of modern times seem somehow farther away, not absent, but less threatening. You think instinctively, when you're there, more of "progress" than of "problems," of "action" and "accommodation" rather than of "confrontation" and "stalemate." Phrases like "civic pride" come to mind and you know that working there will be fun and that something will happen as a result. You have confidence in Kansas City.

Precisely at a time when too many American cities have become places of fear and anger and decay and hope-sapping ugliness, Kansas City still has about it a miraculous sense of normalcy, an everyday life texture which invokes a powerful nostalgia for the optimism and innocence of our mythic past. If you believe in old-fashioned American values, Kansas City is a pretty darned good place to live, work and raise a family.

At the same time, if you care and know anything about cities, you also know that it didn't just get this way "for nothin'." Kansas City is the way it is today because people — smart, determined people — have been caring about it, worrying, arguing, planning, working, doing something about it for a long time. Like all memorable cities, it is the creation of committed citizens, its quality achieved through a fortunate alchemy of energy, vision, will, coalescence, and circumstance over time. Good cities just don't happen; they're good for good reasons, the most important of which are vision, leadership, and care.

If Kansas City is as good as I think it is, then there are important lessons in its history as well as important civic heroes and heroines. For civic history has to do with critical decisions made at critical moments by a few people who are able to take a long term view in evaluating various courses of action; it is also about everyday people who live and carry forward a city's value system. And while most of Kansas City's lessons are generic (they can be applied to many other places) the stories of the individual decision makers and those who,

in their everyday lives, merely carried "history" along, are unique.

As a town planner, I believe that the critical lessons which have led to Kansas City's present, healthy physical structure all point to the value of:

- Powerful, intelligent, vocal, and farsighted local leadership;
- Strong, independent newspapers which know how to identify and promote issues of outstanding public benefits;
- Gifted local and outside consultants;
- Well-conceived, well-illustrated, and well-promoted city-wide plans with both specific spokespersons and well-organized community group support;
- Gifted, inventive, and flexible legal counsel in key city positions;
- Generous local philanthropists and inventive entrepreneurs;
- A pervasive social optimism which is carried by the citizenry and gives a sense of common purpose, consensus and civic morale;
- Nationally recognized models of excellence to emulate;
- Staying power — enough time in elective or appointive office and private sector positions of power to accomplish necessarily long term projects;
- Sound designs (and designers) for public places, buildings, and infrastructure, which age well;
- Attractive available land and the good sense to identify underutilized assets (the job of town planners as well as civic leaders);
- Commitment and will over time — what amounts to a passion for the city at large;
- Getting it done rather than just talking about it;
- A sound (not boom or bust) economy; and
- Good luck.

Good cities in the United States are those that find ways to strike and hold that fragile balance between *communal benefits* and the *public costs* of these to the private citizen. Their leadership is about learning how to pay now for future rewards. In short, cities and leaders and citizens are supposed to find ways to live up to their own expectations and promise. This is the way to keep "everything up to date." And, Kansas City seems, over the years, to have done this pretty well.

— Jaquelin T. Robertson
FAIA AICP

PROLOGUE

In the beginning, the land at the bend of two rivers was magnificent: rocky bluffs crowned with forests of hickory, oak and walnut lifted above a green river plain with upland meadows beyond, rolling away to a broad horizon. Nomadic peoples wandered through the area trapping and fishing. Until Europeans began to settle the wilderness in the early nineteenth century, the region had known no permanent settlements except for a few small villages of mound-dwelling Indians hundreds of years before.

Then fur traders discovered that the confluence of the two rivers made a fine base of operations. In 1821, sons of the powerful merchants, the Chouteau family, came up river from St. Louis to establish a small French-speaking, fur-trading settlement. Other settlers began to come by river and by wagon for land, drawn to eastern Jackson County for its fine forests and tillable soil. Independence, Missouri was platted in 1827 and soon became a center for trade and for outfitting expeditions bound for Santa Fe and other points west.

In 1834, not quite a day's wagon-ride along the trail southwest of Independence, John McCoy filed a plat for a town he called West Port because he envisioned it as a gateway to the west. The store he had opened in 1831 had a brisk trade going with Indians, trappers, traders, muleskinners, wagon bosses, pioneers and anyone else who wanted provisions before leaving civilization. Soon other businesses moved in and made West Port a thriving merchant center.

McCoy and some fellow businessmen could see that a river connection would be a boon, so when Gabriel Prudhomme's farm, with its natural landing on the Missouri River, came up for sale, the men formed the Kansas Town Company and bought it. In 1838, they platted the Town of Kansas and began to work on a road from the landing (at the foot of what is now Grand Avenue), across the high bluffs and rutted terrain to West Port.

Both river and overland trade were successful, but the new Town of Kansas was limited to the levee and a scraggly row of buildings crowded against the stony bluffs covered with timber and underbrush. Roads to the top were cart tracks up natural gullies. Blasting gradually leveled the townsite, but the unattractive results were raw, muddy roads through deep ravines with rough buildings perched on either side.

For a over a decade, the town's reputation was as rugged as its appearance. Saloons and hostelries served a largely transient population in a town so lawless that even outlaws were shocked. But settlers came in droves, brought by the promises of western gold and silver rushes or wide-open land to farm. Many saw the opportunity near the City of Kansas (as it was called after 1853) and stayed.

In 1854, as the fledgling city was beginning to prosper, the Kansas Territory was opened for settlement and the "free state" or "slave state" conflict began in earnest. Because both Southerners and New Englanders had settled the region in considerable numbers, a basic philosophical division was part of the community, and in the eleven years that followed, it tore the region apart. The Civil War began early and finished late along the border of Kansas and Missouri. Guerrilla fighting and formal hostilities ravaged the area. Farms and businesses were destroyed, the spirit of cooperation needed to confront the challenges of life in the region was extinguished, and progress came to a halt.

When the war was officially over, and the area faced the arduous task of rebuilding, businesspeople agreed that only one thing could save Kansas City: railroads. The obstacle to going ahead with train tracks through the city and west was the Missouri River, turbulent, unpredictable and never-before successfully bridged. Before a bridge could even be attempted, congressional approval was required. During the war, much of the commercial life of the region had shifted to Leavenworth and St. Joseph, upriver towns that also wanted bridges and railroads.

Through diligent lobbying and some fancy dealing on the part of Congressman Robert T. Van Horn, Kansas City civic leader and former mayor, permission for the bridge was slipped past the Kansas congressional delegation. The all-important bridge was lost to Leavenworth and secured for Kansas City. Engineer Octave Chanute persisted through two failed sets of footings until he struck upon an innovative bridge design that worked. In 1869, a joyful crowd of thousands welcomed the first train across the Hannibal Bridge. Within three years, Kansas City became the transportation hub connecting the established eastern United States with the promise of a western destiny.

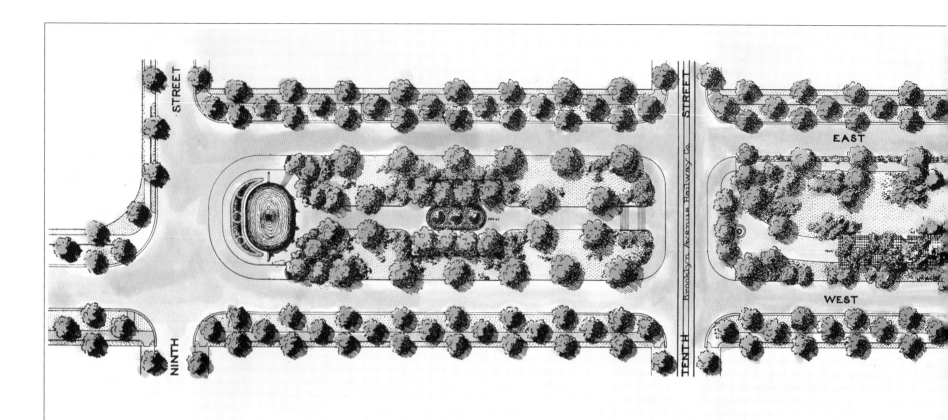

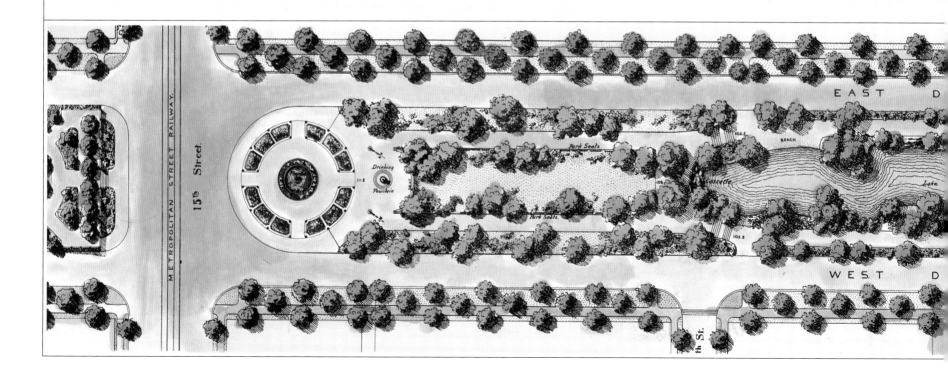

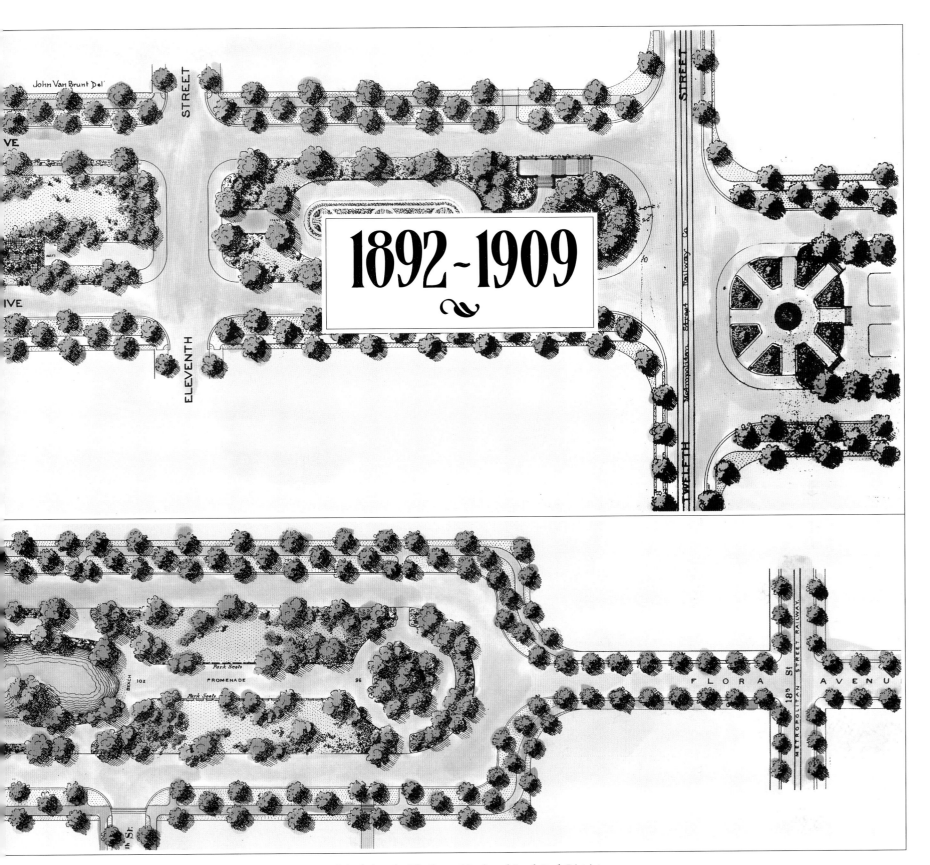

Original plans for The Paseo, North and South Park Districts

Once called Shelter House No. 1, the large limestone building near Swope Park's main gate at Swope Parkway and Meyer Boulevard was designed by Adriance Van Brunt who served on the first Park Board. Today it serves as an administrative building which houses Boulevard Services.

CHAPTER I

A Promising Beginning

ough-hewn Kansas City clung precariously to the bluffs of the Missouri River in the years after 1869. The steep hills that rose abruptly from the river banks were covered with ramshackle houses, dead trees, saloons and plenty of mud.

New arrivals coming by rail were treated to a hair-raising ride on a rickety trolley that travelled up a steep incline on elevated tracks from the river bottoms to the bluff and Main Street. From the river landing, the cart trail up the bluffs into town was almost as scary. Despite these drawbacks, new residents were drawn to the city by the thousands, some intending to stay, others planning to go on but changing their minds when they assessed the rigors of traveling farther west as opposed to the opportunities the bustling little community offered. From 4,000 residents in 1865, Kansas City grew to 32,000 in 1870 and close to 60,000 by 1880, making it one of the largest cities west of the Mississippi River.

It was, however, a city out of control, unsightly and disorderly, with homes, stores, factories, breweries, even packing houses jammed into the few square miles between the Missouri River on the north and the Kansas River bottoms to the west, Thirty-second Street on the south and Cleveland Avenue on the east. Sidewalks were boards; unpaved streets kept the city muddy or dusty depending on the weather; there were no parks or neighborhood playgrounds.

Early Kansas City was a terrific place to make money. Many entrepreneurs seized opportunities in grain, livestock, banking, distribution and retail and established lifestyles that rivaled those of the East Coast's wealthy and upper middle classes. But the luxury and distinction of their homes rarely extended beyond their gates. Middle class neighborhoods were planned by developers for ready access to the public trolley and cable car lines rather than for pleasant living conditions. Poorer workers, the new immigrants and the unemployed crowded into tenements in the neighborhoods left behind by the well-to-do as they moved to newly fashionable districts and ever-larger homes.

Scattered throughout the city were patches of blatant poverty where people lived in ramshackle houses, shanty towns, even tent villages. Zoning was unheard of and no proposal that limited commercial use of land had a chance. Most early attempts at creating civic order through beauty or family recreation fizzled and died. Citizens weren't interested in taxes for improvements, and in the nationally booming real estate market of the 1880s, property was a commodity not to be beautified but to be sold at a profit. Business leaders countered criticism of their city's aesthetic shortcomings by pointing to its astonishing prosperity.

Confronting these issues was less a matter of leadership than of setting priorities. Kansas City had strong leaders, but their primary focus had been securing the town's economic future after the devastation of the Civil War. They had not set out to tackle "quality of life" in the growing city. Then William Rockhill Nelson came to town.

When Nelson arrived from Fort Wayne, Indiana, in 1880 with his mind made up to build a successful newspaper, he cast a critical eye on his newly adopted city. Soon after, he fired the first warning shot in what was soon to become a raging local battle over the importance of urban amenities.

"The pinching economy, the picayunish policy, the miserable parsimony, which characterize our city government must be abandoned," he wrote in an early issue of his evening paper, the *Kansas City Star*. "Kansas City needs good streets, good sidewalks, good sewers, decent public buildings, better street lights, more fire protection, a more efficient police and many other things."

The idea that the highest purpose of cities was to make life better was a radical departure from the goal of land owners and businessmen who believed the first order of business was lining their own pockets. But Nelson had time and ink. For thirty-five years, as editor of the city's most popular paper, Nelson crusaded for civic improvement with an emphasis on parks and boulevards and well-developed neighborhoods. At first he alienated readers. Then people began to agree with him.

On his own property in the Brush Creek Valley, he practiced

The West Bluffs at the turn of the century (top) seemed an unredeemable eyesore: ramshackle buildings, seen here from Thirteenth Street, cascaded down the rough hill toward the river bottoms. Part of George Kessler's 1893 Plan called for making this area a park and by 1921 (bottom), the stone lookouts of West Terrace Park overlooked natural outcroppings and broad drives that gave a fine view of the city's commercial enterprises located in the West Bottoms below.

what he preached, building quality houses on land edged with low limestone rubble walls; laying out streets on contour courses; and planting rambler roses, weigela, and rows and rows of trees. Today the Nelson-Atkins Museum of Art and the University of Missouri-Kansas City owe their lovely settings to Nelson's powerful attachment to land and to nineteenth century ideas of urban beauty.

Though many opposed him and his crusade, Nelson's vision was shared by a number of influential civic leaders including millionaire smelting plant owner August R. Meyer. Born in St. Louis and educated in Europe, Meyer was a metallurgist who had established a modern ore reduction works in California Gulch, Colorado, and helped incorporate the little town of Leadville less than a year before silver was discovered there. The Silver Rush boosted the town's population from 300 to 30,000 in three years. In those years, Meyer made his own fortune, and in 1881, he left Colorado to establish a smelting company in the Argentine area of Kansas City, Kansas.

He settled his family in a home in the fashionable northeast section of Kansas City, and on early morning horseback rides along the bluffs of the Missouri River, he pondered the importance of enjoying natural beauty within a city's limits. He conceived the idea of a boulevard to the bluffs, culminating in a drive through a park there. Meyer's ideas seemed extravagant even to Nelson.

A vigorous social and civic leader with a sophisticated view of urban life and its amenities, Meyer eloquently pushed his ideas for the city of the future. He urged the Commercial Club, forerunner of the Chamber of Commerce, to see social action and civic responsibility as corollaries to economic development. "A period of activity has suddenly transformed a village into a city," he said. "We have attracted a large population and we fail to realize that this change imposes entirely new conditions and brings new problems." Meyer believed the answer to these problems did not lie with more people, more outside capital and expanded manufacturing. Instead, the city needed to develop its citizens' human faculties through education, good city planning and beautification.

Other leaders heard his message and agreed. "Make Kansas City a good place to live in" became their unofficial slogan. Considering the condition of the city at that time, this rallying cry seemed a shout into the wind. Instead, as the future would prove, the slogan reflected fairly the vision and courage of the city's early champions of open spaces and boulevards.

While these men spoke of urban beauty, a young landscape architect was trying to make a living designing it. George E. Kessler

came to the Kansas City area on the heels of both Nelson and Meyer but, unlike them, not to an assured position of civic leadership. He had a job, at the age of twenty, with the Kansas City, Fort Scott and Memphis Railroad Company to design, build and supervise a railway amusement park in Merriam, Kansas. He did the job well, transforming a corner of rolling eastern Kansas prairie into a lovely pleasure ground with a small zoo.

The park was 40 acres bounded on the east by what is now Grandview, three blocks west of Antioch; on the north by Shawnee Mission Parkway; on the south by Sixty-fifth street and on the west by the train tracks east of Merriam Drive. While working on the commission, Kessler lived with his sister and mother on a nearby combined farm and nursery owned by Mrs. Kessler (in what is now Sherwood Forest). In 1900, he married Ida Grant and moved to Kansas City.

Born in Frankenhausen, Germany, George Kessler came to the United States as a child but returned to his native country to study landscape architecture and civil engineering. He first served a two-year apprenticeship at the grand ducal gardens of Weimar; then he studied forestry, botany, and civil engineering under the auspices of the University of Jena; and finally he pursued technical engineering studies at the Gartner-Jehranstalt at Potsdam, capping it all off with a year of travel throughout Europe. "Of all of it," he later said, "the travel was of most value."

Back in this country, he worked for six or eight months in New York City at LeMoult's, a seed company and florist in the Bowery, doing floral arrangements. During this brief period, he corresponded with Frederick Law Olmsted, the American-born luminary in the field of landscape architecture. Olmsted, who maintained a firm in Boston, was an urban reformer of genuine stature in that day. He saw parks as a way to cure society's ills, with natural landscapes restoring the worn-down spirits of city-bound people. In his letters to Kessler, Olmsted offered advice and suggested books the young man should read.

But, most significant to Kansas City's development, Olmsted put Kessler in touch with one of his upstate New York residential clients, H. H. Hunniwell, an executive of the Kansas City, Fort Scott and Gulf Railway Company. Hunniwell hired Kessler for the Merriam railway park job.

Not long after its opening, the Merriam park began to attract crowds of sightseers from Kansas City as well as attention from Kansas City's newspapers. In fact, the park proved so popular that the town changed its name from Campbellton to Merriam to match the name of the park.

The deep ravine dividing Gillham Road between Thirty-sixth and Thirty-fourth streets was transformed by George Kessler in the late nineteenth century at the request of home owners in the Hyde Park area. Today, it is one of Kansas City's cameo parks.

At a picnic in Budd Park in 1907 children and adults enjoyed sloping green spaces interspersed with groves of large trees. The original twenty acres of the park, given to the city in 1891 by lawyer Azariah Budd, were at first under the management of the Board of Public Works and later came into the park board's responsibility.

Scarritt Point in North Terrace Park, which overlooks the Missouri River valley, was named for Nathan Scarritt, founder of the Melrose Methodist Church, whose first home on this site was a log cabin he built himself. Scarritt Point is connected to Prospect Point by Cliff Drive, one of the loveliest drives in the city.

Soon property owners in the city wanted Kessler to do their landscaping. He responded by opening an office for a private practice in the Security Building at Sixth and Wyandotte Streets. Until 1897, however, he also continued to supervise the Merriam park.

The most impressive achievement of his private practice was the beautification of Hyde Park between Thirty-sixth and Thirty-ninth Streets on Gillham Road. Hyde Park was one of the first fashionable suburbs, developed as wealthy residents tired of the stench of the stockyards and the factories visible from the west bluffs and began to move away from the center city. In Hyde Park, owners of the newly built mansions worried about the rough gully at their doorsteps along Gillham Road. Kessler converted the rocky ravine and its tangled brush into a tasteful parkway. The positive effect of his work on real estate values in the Hyde Park neighborhood did not go unnoticed.

Among those who observed Kessler's success was August Meyer. He had just completed a magnificent Elizabethan mansion on eight-and-one-half acres at Forty-fourth Street and Warwick Boulevard in Nelson's Southmoreland development and he needed someone to landscape the grounds. In December, 1891, Meyer wrote Kessler asking him to begin grading and smoothing the ground around the house so it would "settle through the winter and be ready for planting in the spring."

As Kessler worked to develop his private practice, he kept a sharp eye on the maneuverings for public parks. Civic leaders were pushing hard for green spaces within the city, using the rationale that Kansas City must have parks because other cities had them.

Early efforts to do something serious about the issue of parks date from the 1870s when the City Council engaged a workhouse crew to grade the site of the Old Graveyard at Missouri and Oak Streets. The dead were moved to Union Cemetery and a citizens' group tried to organize a city-wide fundraising effort to make the old cemetery into a public park. The result was disappointing, and later, after a legal battle, the original owners regained the cemetery parkland. However, the effort awakened the citizenry to the importance of parks. Soon the city had two.

In 1882, the daughter of Andrew Drips, who had been a trapper and agent for the American Fur Company, deeded to the city a tiny triangle of land at Sixteenth Street and Belleview Road for Kansas City's first park. Originally the land was known as West Prospect Triangle. In 1951, the board changed the name to Andrew Drips Park and dedicated a monument to the trapper.

The last will of attorney Azariah Budd, in 1890, gave the city its second park (twenty acres at St. John and Brighton Avenue) on the condition the city pay his widow $3,000 annually. For 23 years the park was under the management of the Board of Public Works. In 1913, the park board brought an expanded twenty-six acre Budd Park into the park system because Van Brunt Boulevard and the Budd Park Esplanade provided a link to North Terrace Park.

The structure of Kansas City's government was changing in the 1880s and 1890s as the growing city struggled to find a form of government suitable to managing increasingly complex urban problems. Supporters of the push for parks saw an opportunity in the evolving city charter. They worked diligently for an amendment to the charter to allow a politically independent park board. They also worked for state legislation, because the city could not issue bonds for civic improvement without the approval of the legislature.

In 1889, the city's first home rule charter provided for a Board of Park Commissioners, but gave the board no authority to acquire land. A subsequent park law, drafted by attorney John K. Cravens, permitted the mayor, city council and county court to name a park board and empower it to sell bonds of up to one million dollars with approval of two-thirds of the voters. City and county counselors warned that the park law was probably unconstitutional. Nonetheless, the county court appointed two members; Mayor Joseph J. Davenport appointed two; and the mayor himself served as the fifth member of the board.

On May 31, 1890, George Kessler sent a letter of application to this board for the position of landscape architect. However, in January, 1891, the Missouri Supreme Court declared the park law unconstitutional and the board ceased to exist.

A Municipal Improvement Association with August Meyer as president was organized to educate citizens and get out the vote on improvement issues. After a brief but intense campaign by this group, voters amended the city charter to give Kansas City a park board with power to issue city bonds. The mayor was given responsibility for appointing all members. Mayor Nehemiah Holmes immediately named to the board Simeon B. Armour, of the Armour Meat Packing Company; William C. Glass, a retired wholesale liquor dealer and realtor; Louis Hammerslough, a prominent clothing merchant; Adriance Van Brunt, an architect; and August Meyer, whom he named president of the board.

Of all of these, Hammerslough probably best exemplified the general response to the need for parks: once an adversary of beautification as an unnecessary expense, he became a staunch

Three rows of trees (two on the parking and one behind the sidewalk) planted at the direction of George Kessler along Admiral Boulevard at the turn of the century grew to provide both shade and beauty for the thoroughfare.

Before it became the jewel of the Kansas City boulevard system, The Paseo was a ten-block-long strip of poor homes and run-down buildings.

Gentlemen   Ans'd   Page City, Mo,
              May 6.97   May 4th 1897,
              Do you want any
squirrels?   If you do please write
and let me know what you are
willing to pay for them, I can
furnish you some right away
if you need them
              Very Resp't Lee Martin
                          Page City, Mo.

Hearing of the new Kansas City park system, a nearby farmer offered to provide something every park needs: squirrels. Park board minutes do not reveal whether or not he made a sale.

supporter. A German Jewish immigrant, Hammerslough had sold his hugely successful clothing business, bought the area's German-language newspaper and renamed it the *Kansas City Globe.* In a series of dueling editorials, Hammerslough and Nelson fought about park plans. Gradually, Hammerslough came to believe in the desirability of parks and put his energy behind Nelson's campaign.

When the city elected a new mayor, William S. Cowherd, in the spring of 1892, he reappointed Holmes' five men. Together they set an example for all the boards to follow in the next one hundred years.

ॐ

The 1893 Report:
Blueprint for an Historic System

At the first meeting of the new board on March 8, 1892, the members voted to enter into discussion with the F. L. Olmsted firm of Boston regarding a parks and boulevard system for Kansas City.

Olmsted was one of the 19th century's great landscape architects and had been this country's leading authority on parks since 1858. His name was virtually synonymous with efforts to create natural environments within urban settings. He had designed Chicago's Jackson Park, Boston's Franklin Park and Brooklyn's Prospect Park, as well as Central Park in New York City, his best known work.

Seventy years old in 1892, Olmsted was in failing health and, although his reputation was solid, the firm's other landscape architects were handling new business. One of those associates, Henry Sargent Codman, was sent to Kansas City to assess the situation. He visited the city briefly late in April, gathered data on population and taxable values, and sent back a preliminary report in May. No action was taken by the board on his report; shortly afterward, Codman died.

George Kessler applied to this new board for the position of landscape architect. The board couldn't really afford his design services but hired him to be secretary to the board at a salary of $100 a month. Kessler also agreed to serve as engineer to the board without pay. This strange hiring served the interests of both Kessler and the weakly-funded park board. The board did not pay him for his early planning work, but they gave him the chance to do the work and that is what mattered to Kessler.

For months, he and August Meyer exchanged ideas about urban beauty, as Kessler studied Kansas City's topography and then began to design a park and boulevard system that would embrace the entire city. Kessler and Meyer agreed, "it is far better to plan comprehensively and broadly and proceed with actual construction leisurely, than to attempt economy in the system."

In March 1893, Olmsted himself made a trip to Kansas City while working in Chicago on the World's Columbian Exposition. Meyer took him around the city and showed him how Kessler's plans for parks and boulevards would tie the city together. Correspondence records that Olmsted approved of the plans "in the main," but urged the board to alter them to include a large urban park of the kind the Olmsted firm had designed for other cities.

Meyer rejected this idea. He believed Kessler's plans contained better solutions to the "peculiar conditions" that existed within the boundaries of Kansas City.

Outlined in final form, the 1893 Report of the Board had three sections: Meyer's letter to the mayor; his recommendations as president of the board; and Kessler's designs, photographs, and maps of the rugged topography of Kansas City to illustrate his treatise on how the board's recommendations could be implemented. Kessler did not shrink from the challenge of the steep hills and river bluffs, the creek beds and gorges, which had given early city developers so many headaches. He saw them as aesthetic assets and he translated to paper his vision of a system of boulevards that would curve gracefully as they followed easy grades to end in three large parks: one on the West Bluffs, one on the North Bluffs and one on the site of the especially ugly Penn Street ravine.

For a long time citizens had complained about the West Bluffs where weatherbeaten shacks looked as if they might at any moment slide off the hills into the river or onto the tracks below. Kansas Citians were embarrassed knowing that arrivals to the Union Depot would form a first impression of them as poor civic housekeepers. Kessler's idea was to clear the bluffs of unsightly structures and then build retaining walls and steps that would blend with the natural stone of the terrace. He also designed strategic lookout points that afforded panoramic viewing of the city's vigorous life in its manufacturing and transportation center, the West Bottoms.

The citizenry also had a poor opinion of the North Bluffs, a site they described as too rugged for even a goat to climb. But Kessler saw the perfect opportunity there to bring the beauty and serenity of the country into the city. He planned to connect the two existing promontories above the cliffs, Scarritt Point and Prospect Point, with a cliff-side drive that would periodically afford a view of the

This free form wading pool was constructed in the ravine at The Grove in 1911. The Grove with its beautiful native walnut trees is located at an interesting bend in what is now Benton Boulevard near Truman Road.

*Holmes Square was more hospitable to the play of children after the **Kansas City Star** decried the absence of proper playground equipment and the presence of "Keep Off the Grass" signs. In 1907, the outdoor gymnasium was installed and two years later the park board hired a playground director for the summer months.*

river below and give "the impression of being isolated from all habitation and the disturbing intrusions of city life." He then planned to create a Concourse by filling a deep valley with tons of earth so visitors could enjoy a breathtaking view of the Missouri River from a high flat expanse of land. On the Concourse, he planned a Colonnade in the grand tradition of the classical Beaux Art school.

The land in the Penn Street ravine from about Twenty-seventh Street to Twenty-second Street along Broadway was steep and scarred by gullies that ran full after every rain. Kessler found it desirable because it offered a variety of landforms and vistas near the center of the city. Transforming this land into a park, however, called for creative engineering by Kessler. To divert runoff water from higher ground, he planned a system of underground drains and an earth dam, which would create a lake in the northwest section of the park.

He was so successful with this park that, in 1902, the Southlands Land & Improvement Company, a neighborhood group of landowners, and others gave the board the land for Roanoke Park, thirty-seven-and-a-half acres of wooded loveliness at Valentine Road and Roanoke Parkway. The benefactors said they caught "the spirit of conserving nature's beauty before it became marred" from Kessler.

The 1893 Plan also called for three smaller parks — Independence Plaza at Independence Boulevard and Park Avenue; The Grove at Benton Boulevard and Truman Road; and Holmes Square, just south of Truman Road on Holmes — and a large parade ground for organized athletics and military drill. The site selected for The Parade was at the terminus of what would become The Paseo on ground previously used for circus performances, balloon ascensions and other public spectacles so popular at the time.

Kessler considered The Paseo, which he planned to originate at Independence Boulevard, to be a "transition thoroughfare" (something between a park and a boulevard) and a passage from The Parade to the rest of the boulevard system. He designed each block as a unique individual park. Meyer, who had business interests in Mexico, influenced Kessler on the design of The Paseo, which took its name and character from The Paseo de la Reforma, a famous boulevard in Mexico City.

Other boulevards in a system Meyer and Kessler believed would establish, classify and draw together residential sections of the city were Independence, Gladstone and Benton, with plans for Broadway, Linwood, and Armour (at that time still south of the city limits).

The comprehensive and farsighted 1893 Report of the Board of Park Commissioners promised to give Kansas City what soon became its one truly unique feature — the parks and boulevard system designed by Kessler. The final report contained no studies or reports by F.L. Olmsted or any member of his firm, but that has not kept many persons over the years from mistakenly giving Olmsted the credit for designing the system. Olmsted's name was well-regarded. When Kessler designed the Kansas City system, he was all but unknown to the general public, although held in high regard by professional planners.

The Olmsted legend persisted. When the secretary of the Lincoln Park Commissioners in Chicago wrote in 1902 requesting a copy of the "Olmsted report," Kessler answered and tried to untangle the confusion. "We first studied the city very carefully," he wrote, "and made tentative selections of the park and boulevard lines and after thoroughly settling on the system as originally outlined, Mr. Meyer desired the judgement and its resultant support of Mr. F.L. Olmsted Sr. Mr. O . . . visited K.C. and made a report . . . approved in general terms the selections made, suggesting some slight possible additions and beyond that the Olmsteds never had anything to do with the K.C. Park system."

In 1917, Henry D. Ashley, a former park board president, made a public speech in Kansas City giving credit to Olmsted for the Kansas City system. The board's first attorney, D.J. Haff, answered him on May 10, "I have investigated the matter, and I find that Mr. Olmstead [sic] spent exactly two days in Kansas City, as a guest of Mr. Meyer, and no more, and that was after the plans had been made by Mr. Meyer and Mr. Kessler, and maps had been prepared, park areas selected, routes for boulevards determined and topographic surveys made. Naturally it is a matter of great injustice to Mr. Kessler to have a former President of the Park Board say that Mr. Olmstead [sic] is entitled to the credit, or any credit in planning Kansas City's park system."

As late as 1962, a booklet "Cowtown 1890 Becomes City Beautiful 1962," prepared for the park board, included a picture of Frederick L. Olmsted and said he had worked with Kessler on the Kansas City system. But despite the mistaken local attribution to Olmsted, Kessler's work gained him a substantial reputation around the country.

In 1901, Kessler began a professional relationship with St. Louis, first as the chief landscape architect for the Louisiana Purchase Exposition and then as director of the restoration of Forest Park, which had been the site of the fair. In 1910, he moved from Kansas City to St. Louis and though he continued to work for the Kansas City park board, he worked in many cities in the years that followed.

The public bath at The Grove at Benton Boulevard and Truman Road, an outdoor swimming pool built in 1911 and used primarily by men and boys, was known as the Roman Bath.

When it was first built, the western third of The Grove was set aside for the gentler outdoor sports of women and children, such as maypole dancing, while the eastern third was used for the rougher sports of boys and men, such as baseball.

Washington Square north of Admiral Boulevard had one of the first wading pools built by the park board.

The drinking fountain at Sixteenth Street and The Paseo (shown here in 1908) was easier to reach with the addition of a stone on the top step.

In the early years of this century, the Blue River in eastern Kansas City was used by boaters (above left) and even had a boat club located near Fifteenth Street (left). Today the river is appreciated for its natural beauty even as it is cursed for its occasional flooding. A flood control project begun in 1991 under the direction of the Corps of Engineers will eliminate this threat but the look of the river will also be altered.

Turn of the century elegance in Kansas City was best expressed in the graceful pergola, between Tenth and Eleventh Streets, designed for pedestrian strolling along The Paseo, shown here in 1900.

William Rockhill Nelson used his newspaper, the **Kansas City Star** *to convince the community that parks and boulevards were necessary. In the century that has followed, the* **Star** *has continued to support the parks and boulevards, rallying public enthusiasm, showcasing achievements, and helping the community mindful of the value of green spaces.*

The Paseo's Ninth Street fountain, shown under construction in 1899, will become the Women's Leadership fountain, with restoration financed by the Central Exchange.

Leaders of growing cities such as Denver, Dallas, Memphis, Houston and El Paseo wanted him to give their communities the same urban beauty he had given Kansas City. In 1921, two years before Kessler's death, the University of Missouri conferred on him an honorary doctorate degree.

After he died, the park board decided to name a short road near the Liberty Memorial after Kessler. When Frank Vaydik came to Kansas City to be park director in 1964, he was disturbed by the city's apparent lack of appreciation of Kessler, who had earned a national reputation as a pioneering park planner. The board decided to rename North Terrace Park for Kessler. Residents of the northeast neighborhoods objected because, they said, Kessler was only an employee of the park department and not deserving of such an honor. They wanted the park to be named for the Rev. Nathan Scarritt, original owner of the land.

"You'll always have trouble naming anything after someone who was in the administration and who was not elected to office," recalled R.E. Soper, who was board secretary at the time. "And that's what happened. People objected to renaming North Terrace for that reason. They came into the board meeting and said in no uncertain terms, 'Kessler was paid for what he did.' But what he did was so great!"

On July 6, 1971, nearly fifty years after his death, park board members Harold Holliday, Jr., Carl Migliazzo and president Dr. Robert H. Hodge passed a resolution stating that Kessler had never been honored properly for his great contribution to the beauty of Kansas City. They officially renamed North Terrace "Kessler Park."

Besides the anguish caused Kessler, the misunderstanding surrounding Olmsted's role in Kansas City is unfortunate for two other reasons. First of all, it obscures the fact that German landscape architects of that period, particularly Peter Joseph Lenne of Berlin, had far more influence on Kessler than did Olmsted. "Nineteenth century German landscape architects reflected the influence of the preceding period," said Kurt Culbertson, an Aspen, Colorado, landscape architect and biographer of Kessler, "when they used a combination of the natural and the formal." The design for The Paseo and The Colonade at Kessler Park especially show Kessler's blending of the natural landscape with classically designed forms.

The confusion over Olmsted's role also has prevented recognition of the influence of August Meyer on the designs for the Kansas City system. Although he was not an architect, Meyer was an engineer, and something of a Renaissance man in his wide interests. Like Kessler, he had been given a European education by German

parents. These two men must have felt very much in tune with each other as they worked and planned Kansas City's green spaces. The success of their collaboration is evident in the enduring grace and style of the parks and boulevards system.

The Fourth Key Man

Without the goading of Nelson, the leadership of Meyer, and the vision of Kessler, Kansas City never would have had its 1893 Plan. Without the legal mind of the board's attorney, D. J. Haff, the system of parks and boulevards might have stayed a dream on paper, never built.

Haff made Meyer's job as park board president much easier and Meyer gave him the credit he deserved. "The law upon which rests the entire structure of our park work was the child of your brain and its nurture into vigorous youth is due to your sleepless care," he wrote to Haff.

The law Meyer had in mind was the 1895 amendment to the city charter which granted the park board both administrative and fiscal independence. The board as it was first established in 1892 could plan but it could do little else because of funding restrictions. To solve the financial problems, Haff proposed that the board be authorized to sell park certificates to financial institutions to pay for property already selected for park purposes. Since the board would immediately receive the face value of the certificates, it could pay owners in full for condemned land and get right to work.

Kansas Citians wanted the parks and boulevard system designed by Kessler but they were naturally apprehensive about whether or not the city was overextending itself to pay for the improvements. Haff's proposals to sell park certificates made sense and, at a city election in 1895, the citizens gave the charter amendment a ten-to-one margin of approval. The next year, the Supreme Court declared the amendment constitutional and the park certificates valid.

In addition to providing a solution to the financing problem, Haff also took care of the park board's trouble with the Board of Public Works. The earlier charter amendment required all park work to be approved first by Public Works and the results were bureaucratic delays and disagreements. Haff freed the park board from this bottleneck by omitting any mention of the Board of Public Works in the new amendment. Meyer and his fellow board members were enormously grateful to Haff for that legal maneuver.

When streets were packed dirt, dust was a major problem and boulevard services included sprinkling the roadways. Fringed harnesses looked festive and also helped keep flies away.

A loafing place for juvenile delinquents known as "Razor Park" was transformed by park crews into a charming playground for children, complete with a spring fed lake. The first 27 acres of the more than 32-acre Spring Valley Park were acquired in 1902.

The transplanting of a fourteen foot maple tree at Thirteenth Street and The Paseo was a major undertaking in 1904.

A farm boy from Michigan, Delbert J. Haff visited Kansas and Missouri in the early 1880s while selling books to finance a college education. He liked what he saw in Kansas City and after graduating from the University of Michigan law school in 1886, he moved to town and opened a law office in the Underwriters' Exchange Building at Sixth and Wyandotte Streets, not far from the office of George Kessler. He was soon caught up in the life of the growing community, and in 1890 he authored the legislative act that established park districts in the city. After the creation of the park board, he became its first attorney and fought the board's legal battles during those turbulent early years.

From 1892 to 1900, park opponents fought the board tenaciously. After the 1895 amendment passed, the opponents formed a Taxpayers' League to try to scuttle park plans. The *Kansas City Journal* joined their cause and editorially challenged all park business, including whether August Meyer should serve on the board since his home was in Westport, still at the time a separate town, although he also maintained a residence at the Kansas City Club. The *Kansas City Star* countered by making park opponents members of a facetious "Hammer and Padlock Club," suggesting that the League wanted a padlock on the city's pocket book and planned to hammer at anything resembling progress.

Nelson's voice in the community was credible and his ridicule of the Taxpayer's League was effective. After years of wrangling, the opposition began to weaken because it could offer no alternative to Kessler's plan. As beauty began replacing ugliness along Independence and Gladstone Boulevards, in North Terrace Park, and along The Paseo, more and more Kansas Citians became excited about the parks and boulevards system.

The changing tide of public opinion didn't keep the Taxpayers' League from testing the constitutionality of the 1895 amendment in the courts for more than four years, but the Supreme Court never deviated from its original opinion. In 1900, when the Court rejected all arguments in a case involving the condemnation process for land for the North Terrace Park, opponents of the parks finally admitted defeat.

In 1909, Haff became president of a park board reduced in size to three members by another change in the city charter. He was only midway through his term when a mayoral candidate, Henry Jost, called for a "little less of art and more of practical sense" and Haff responded that Jost's election would be a "public calamity." After Jost was elected mayor in 1912, he replaced Haff with General Cusil Lechtman, president of a printing company, saying "I told General Lechtman I wanted a business administration of the Park Board. If there is one department of the city that needs the pruning knife and can most easily bear it, that department is the Park division."

Fortunately, the magnificent plan was well on its way to fruition by this time, due in large measure to Haff's innovative leadership. The park board's first attorney lived to see a grateful city dedicate a bronze bust of him on October 27, 1940, at Haff Circle, west of the main entrance to Swope Park.

❧

The Unbelievable Gift

When the parks and boulevard system was in the planning stage, August Meyer turned aside F. L. Olmsted's suggestion that the city needed a large urban park, partly because no appropriate parcel of land was readily available. Then in June 1896, in a gesture that startled everyone, Colonel Thomas H. Swope, of Independence, gave the community 1,324 acres of land, four miles south of the city limits.

Swope's gift had three conditions: the land was to be named for him; it was to be used as a park forever; and the park board was required to spend at least $5,000 a year for ten years for its improvement.

Shy and mysterious, Swope was an enigmatic character in Kansas City's early history. An Easterner who had come to Kansas City in 1856, he had made a fortune in real estate. He owned vast holdings in Kansas City that were, of course, subject to taxation. He had been a vocal detractor of public improvement plans that required increased taxes to pay for them. While his motive for giving so much land may have been entirely altruistic, some people believed Swope may have shrewdly reasoned that the $5,000 a year the board would have to spend improving Swope Park would tie up its resources and slow down other park developments and the potential tax increases associated with them.

Only a few months after his gift, Swope joined the anti-park forces seeking signatures on petitions opposing both West Terrace and North Terrace Parks. In 1897, the anti-park groups launched a campaign against the plan's tax consequences. Petition drives, publicity campaigns and lobbying lasted until 1900, when the parks and boulevards plan was at last secured.

Kansas Citians did not care why Swope had been so generous. They accepted his gift with wild enthusiasm and a day-long jubilee. Although the land was beyond the trolley lines and could not be

UNION CEMETERY

Tucked away in a serene and shaded area just south of Crown Center between Warwick and McGee trafficways are twenty-seven acres of land maintained by the park board, the site of historic Union Cemetery. The quiet beauty of the place absorbs so much of the noise of cars that, once inside the cemetery gates, one notices only the natural sounds of birds and wind in the trees.

Cemetery founders chose the site, halfway between Westport and the Town of Kansas, in 1857. Named for the union between the two small communities, the cemetery land seemed to the founders to be spacious enough to serve both communities for all time.

From the beginning, Union Cemetery had problems. More space was soon needed. Other cemeteries were established and the competition increased financial difficulties which required selling off much of the original forty-nine acres. Burials took place until 1888, when health officers closed the cemetery, claiming health hazards. Historians speculate that those claims may have been manufactured because a number of Kansas City businessmen coveted the land for its prime location. In fact, burials resumed some years later and continue, although rarely, today.

Its name leads many to presume that Union loyalists established the cemetery, but, in fact, soldiers from both the Union and the Confederacy are

buried there. One grave contains the remains of Rebel soldiers wounded and captured during the Battle of Westport, who died as prisoners of war. Veterans of every other American war also rest in Union Cemetery.

The board especially treasures Union Cemetery because of its historic value. Those buried in the cemetery include many early citizens of the Town of Kansas, later to become Kansas City. Dr. Johnston Lykins, the first mayor of the Town of Kansas, is buried there, as is his widow who later married the artist George Caleb Bingham. When Bingham died, he left instructions to bury his body in the cemetery facing south, contrary to the custom of burying the dead facing east because they wouldn't see God if their backs were turned. Bingham said he believed the Lord would find him no matter which way he faced.

After assuming responsibility for the cemetery in 1937, the park board refurbished the little house at Twenty-eighth and Main Streets, which belonged to the cemetery and was known as Sexton's Cottage. Later, with the help of Mrs. Robert Hodge, it was furnished with authentic 1880 antiques. Halloween pranksters burned the house and destroyed the furnishings in 1985. With the help of The National Association of Women Contractors and the engineering firm of Black and Veatch, the park board restored Sexton's Cottage which was dedicated in 1990.

A quiet winter snow in secluded Union Cemetery testifies to the serenity of the burial grounds which were established in 1857 on land that was then halfway between the township of Westport and the Town of Kansas. The cemetery, now well hidden, is within a stone's throw of Crown Center, a bustling residential, retail and office development.

reached except on horseback or in a buggy over country roads, the *Kansas City Star* invited the city to come to the park on June 25, 1896, for a grand day of celebration. Eighteen thousand people showed up, using every imaginable conveyance to reach the park. They spent the day feasting, listening to speeches and concerts, and marveling that their city suddenly had the largest urban park in the country, bigger than even Central Park in New York City.

The park board completed a survey of the park on January 1, 1898. Because the area was so primitive, the board then spent slightly more than the required $5,000 each year for several years just for basic items such as labor, clover seed, wells, pumps, nails, staples and cement.

Since the acceptance of Swope's gift, the park board has added approximately 442 more acres to the original 1,324, making Swope Park the centerpiece of the park's system. The park contains two lakes: the lagoon with its modern-style boathouse and the rustic Lake of the Woods. Before this lake was filled with water, it was a natural basin full of stunted trees and undergrowth. A dam thirty-five feet high and sixty feet long was built to separate it from water flooding from the Blue River.

The park is also the final resting place of Thomas Swope. After his death in 1909, Kansas City architects Wight and Wight designed a memorial consisting of a large pillared stone portal flanked by two guardian lions, carved by sculptor Charles Keck. The park board placed the memorial and Swope's mausoleum on the summit of a hill on the east side of the park and dedicated it in 1917.

Despite Swope Park's ninety-five years as Kansas City's premier park, the vast park has yet to realize its full potential and Kessler's prediction that every portion of the property would be the public's "great pleasure ground." Still ahead is the realization of many long-deferred projects, now scheduled into the board's Second Century plan for the park.

An important visual feature at the north end of The Paseo, The Parade was originally planned as a place for all kinds of outdoor games and military demonstrations and was built on an open field where traveling circuses had been setting up since the 1850s. As the city outgrew it, The Parade became a neighborhood park.

Landmark columns and splendid beds of seasonal blooms at Gregory Boulevard and Ward Parkway along with pieces of statuary and formal flower beds in other locations, punctuate the long sweep of parkway from the Country Club Plaza to Ninety-second Street.

CHAPTER II
The City Beautiful Prototype

In his 1910 report to the park board, George Kessler said, "We are closing an era. The original plan [has been] realized in general and in detail to a degree perhaps without precedence in public works. Land has been secured, progress made on construction, details planned, the finish is assured."

He attributed success to working from a plan that embraced nearly the entire city in a natural setting which he felt was remarkable. "No locality could rival the topographical eccentricities of our city," he said. "They became the basis for a diversified park and boulevard system."

Certainly Kessler and Meyer knew they were breaking new ground with the 1893 Report. When he left the park board in 1901, Meyer wrote Kessler that he believed they had all been "gifted with a poetic vision to create a park system that would have a continuous and potent influence on the business importance and social character of our city." But it is doubtful that either man knew just how profoundly he was influencing future city planners.

The obstacles overcome in Kansas City's long legal and philosophical struggle against park opponents cleared a path for the City Beautiful movement, not only here, but in cities throughout the country. By the turn of the century, most major urban areas in America were aware of a need for comprehensive planning that would give their cities unity and beauty. They knew they had to come to terms with their urban environments, with crowding, industrial pollution and the increasingly ugly circumstances in which most city-dwellers had to live.

The City Beautiful movement came to fruition in the spirit of other progressive reform movements of the late nineteenth and early twentieth centuries. Recognizing that vast numbers of Americans were destined to live permanently without the restorative powers of rural beauty, early urban planners and landscape architects directed their energies toward making life in the cities as convenient, safe and pleasant as possible.

The roots of the City Beautiful movement were in nineteenth century landscape architecture, particularly the work of Frederick Law Olmsted. Though Olmsted did not start the movement, his ideas and those of others, particularly landscape architects trained in Europe, crystallized into a philosophy that provided natural beauty as an answer to the ills of city living.

The World's Columbia Exposition of 1893 in Chicago contributed to the movement with its comprehensive plan for buildings and grounds on a single scale. The success of the Chicago Exposition strongly influenced proponents of the City Beautiful movement to champion park-like settings for public buildings in the civic center of cities.

These planners believed urban environments must have well-located parks coordinated in a park and boulevard system; children must be socialized through team play at attractive playgrounds; streets must be paved; trees must be planted; public buildings must be aesthetically designed and urban sprawl must be controlled.

Kansas City emerged as a leader of this movement because of its bold plan for an interlocking system of parks and boulevards, but Meyer and Kessler had no way to know at the time they proposed the 1893 Plan that they were, in fact, helping lay a foundation for a nationwide beautification movement. They only knew they shared a vision of how life should be lived in an urban environment.

Other landscape planning movements of that time included the Garden City concept and the Country Life movement. Both were responses to the frustrations of urbanization, but these efforts did not rival the influence of the City Beautiful movement because they were so solidly anti-city. In varying ways, they advocated turning away from America's cities to return to rural communities. These movements depended on citizens having the resources to escape city life. The Garden City movement is reflected today in suburban developments around the country; J.C. Nichols' original plan for Mission Hills, Kansas, is one of the best examples. The Country Life movement inspired grand rural retreats such as Longview Farms in

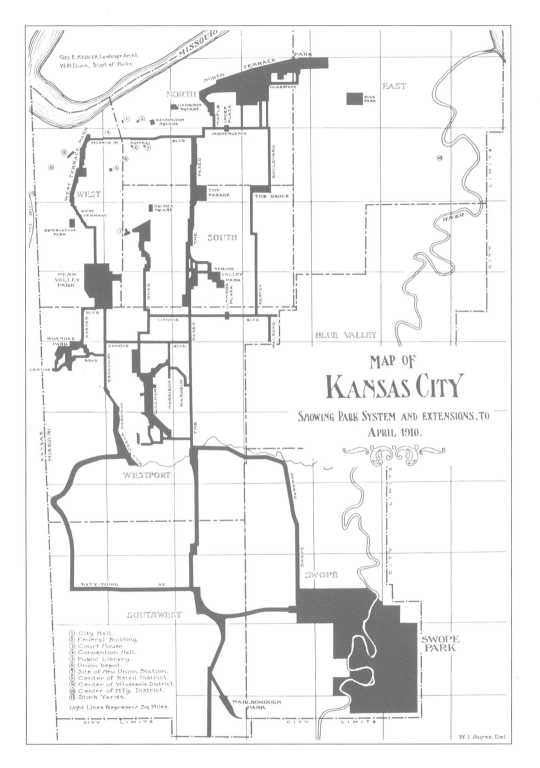

MAP OF
KANSAS CITY
SHOWING PARK SYSTEM AND EXTENSIONS, TO
APRIL 1910.

① City Hall.
② Federal Building.
③ Court House.
④ Convention Hall.
⑤ Public Library.
⑥ Union Depot.
⑦ Site of New Union Station.
⑧ Center of Retail District.
⑨ Center of Wholesale District.
⑩ Center of Mfg. District.
⑪ Stock Yards.

Light Lines Represent Sq. Miles.

In 1910, George Kessler (above) told the park board that the original 1893 plan for parks and boulevards in Kansas City had been realized to a degree "perhaps without precedence in public works." In fewer than twenty years, the board had secured land that tied Kansas City together with graceful boulevards that extended from North Terrace, West Terrace and Penn Valley Parks to Swope Park just inside the southeast limits of the city.

Lee's Summit, Missouri. The City Beautiful movement, on the other hand, advocated making cities livable.

Kansas City in the late nineteenth century was headed toward the urban problems that gave rise to landscape planners' reform ideas. Already a pattern of develop-and-abandon had been established as merchants left the early downtown, around the city market at Fifth and Delaware, for new stores along Grand Avenue south of Ninth Street. Wealthy homeowners left mansions on Knob Hill (about Second and Delaware) and Quality Hill for new homes in Hyde Park. In addition, retail and residential areas were sprinkled with industrial concerns because Kansas City did not have a zoning ordinance until 1923.

However, Kessler and Meyer in their 1893 Plan assured the city a core beauty. As Meyer wrote in that report, "The conditions that we now actually find clearly demand that there be established a strong tendency toward concentration and uniformity of use [through] the establishment of a comprehensive, well-planned and thoroughly maintained system of boulevards [that] will check the tendency to spread out by [building] within the city."

By 1910, Kansas City's well-developed system of boulevards included: Independence, from Dykington to Benton; Gladstone, from Independence to Indian Mound; Maple, from Independence to the west end of Cliff Drive in North Terrace Park; Prospect, from Summit Drive to Cliff Drive; Admiral, from Grand to Independence and Dykington; and The Paseo, from Admiral south to the city limits. Land also had been acquired for Benton from St. John to Swope Parkway.

These thoroughfares connected the different residential districts of the city and established areas of high property value. The picturesque parks brought to life Kessler's vision of "green turf and waving trees," assuring residents a more natural and healthier life in the city. By the first decade of the twentieth century, Kansas City's system of parks and boulevards was the paradigm for all communities seeking the City Beautiful ideal.

❧

Kansas City's Front Door

By the time Kansas City's magnificent new Union Station opened in 1914, the nationwide City Beautiful movement was waning. The construction of the mammoth station may have marked the end of the movement here because the city failed to build a civic and cultural center on land south of the station.

Civic centers were strongly identified with the City Beautiful movement. Advocates of the movement believed that attractively designed public buildings situated in a park setting with wide streets, plazas and open spaces should be an integral part of comprehensive city plans. Since these civic centers ideally would be readily visible to visitors, the area south of the new station seemed ideal for Kansas City's center.

Kansas Citians wanted an attractive entrance to the city. They had been embarrassed too long by the row of what one local journalist called "bum saloons and red hots" along Union Avenue, the first view of the city travellers had when debarking at the old Union Depot. Residents didn't want similar hostelries and taverns on the hillside facing the new station.

The idea for a civic center opposite the station probably originated with Jarvis Hunt, the flamboyant designer of the Union Station. Undoubtedly, the Court of Honor of Chicago's 1893 World's Fair influenced him as it did many designers who saw a civic center as a tangible symbol of pride and spirit.

When the railway terminal company deeded the area south of Union Station to the city (now part of the Liberty Memorial grounds), the park board planned it as a Station Park. Hunt, Kessler and the local landscape architecture firm of Hare & Hare were among a number of architects and designers who submitted plans for a civic and cultural center on park land.

Kessler's concept called for public buildings in groups along six blocks extending from Broadway to Grand Avenue. A high monument on a circular base would serve as the focal point at the intersection of Twenty-fifth and Main Streets directly in front of the station.

Hunt offered a vision of a widened and lowered Main Street with Italian Renaissance buildings in a semi-circle. A huge domed city hall would reign at the center of the curve, a post office and library-art museum would sit on the east, and a county building and a hall of records or armory would anchor the west. Nelson and the *Kansas City Star* supported Hunt's plan, but D.J. Haff, then president of the park board, objected. He believed the low elevation of Union Station would require the city to re-grade Station Park at an estimated cost of $250,000 before buildings could be constructed.

Haff suggested Hunt raise his station ten to twenty feet, but Hunt refused and could not be persuaded; the terminal company had given him the right to negotiate the matter for them. By 1912, without support for his expensive plan, Hunt and the park board agreed to a more modest proposal to smooth and terrace rather than

❧

Formal gardens which defined The Paseo in the early years of the Twentieth century were eliminated after 1940 because of upkeep difficulties.

The Colonnade, set on the top of the ridge at the entrance to North Terrace (now Kessler) Park, is an intriguing example of Kessler's inclination to enhance a natural setting with formal architecture.

re-grade Station Park. The board also proposed connecting Broadway on the west with Gillham Road on the east with a broad trafficway, the present Pershing Road.

During the next several years, Kansas City struggled with its growth and steady modernization. Public welfare became a matter of increasing concern as a burgeoning population intensified requirements for health care, housing, employment, and education. A number of social service agencies, hospitals and schools were begun in the years prior to World War I. Tax dollars and philanthropic gifts were needed to fund these efforts and supporters of city improvements found their focus was necessarily broadened. It was difficult to put beauty before health and welfare. Civic center plans stalled.

Then the war changed everything. Kansas Citians were galvanized by the magnitude of the conflict. For the first time, they shared a worldwide point of view — and a place on the world map. Kansas City's beef and grain and industries such as the garment trade were crucial to the war effort. When companies of local soldiers marched down Grand Avenue every day, awaiting their overseas orders, Kansas City residents felt more and more a part of the national scene. On Armistice Day in 1919, a larger crowd than ever before in the city's history lined a downtown parade route to celebrate the end of the war.

Soon after, 83,000 residents contributed over two million dollars in a matter of weeks to build a monument to peace and to commemorate the men and women who fought and died in World War I. In 1921, during the American Legion National Convention, a memorial site was dedicated — across the street from Union Station. Those present included 100,000 spectators, the Allied Military leaders, Vice-President Calvin Coolidge, and the Supreme Commander of the American Expeditionary Force in France, General John J. Pershing, for whom the street between the station and the monument was later named.

Construction was completed in 1926 on the Liberty Memorial on the crest of the hill opposite Union Station. The park board had enthusiastically endorsed the site and revived the idea of a civic and art center on the mall south of the Memorial. Haff favored this location, saying the center could be another "Trafalgar Square or Place de la Concorde." However, the voters could not be convinced to spend the money needed to create a civic and cultural center on the Memorial mall.

Twenty years later, as part of the ambitious Ten Year plan, citizens did vote bond money to replace the outdated city hall and courthouse at Fifth and Main with modern buildings at Twelfth and Oak, in the heart of downtown. These buildings created a kind of civic center, but hindsight now underscores the unfortunate loss of the public center Kessler and others imagined as Kansas City's grand front door.

An afternoon in the park was an appropriate outing for ladies at the turn of the century.

LAWN
SEATING
SPACE

STAGE

PICNIC AREA
OVENS, INFORMAL BALL
PLAYING, E.T.C.

SHELTER

WILD
GARDEN

55TH STREET

PARKING - 150 CARS

WORNALL

PUTTING GREEN

ROSE GARDEN

SHELTER

PARKING

74 CARS

1910~1939

FORMAL GARDEN

UTILITY BLDG.

PICNIC AREA

MAIN SHELTER

JACOB L. LOOSE
STATUE

SCALE IN FEET

0 50 150 200

Early General Plan for Jacob L. Loose Memorial Park.

The Loose Park lake is popular during the warm weather months with strollers and picnickers and with ice skaters during the winter. In 1864, this serene park was the site of a decisive and bloody installment of the Civil War's Battle of Westport.

When the park board received the gift of Loose Park, it hired Hare & Hare to create a plan, and a young landscape architect, Gordon Whiffen, designed most of the park. Whiffen says the land had only a gravel road running through it. "We pretty much started from scratch," says Whiffen who worked on the driveway, formal panel, shelter building and rose garden. The popular Loose Park lake was also in the early plans.

CHAPTER III
The City Beautiful Ideal Lives On

ong after the City Beautiful movement had faded nationally, one man — real estate entrepreneur J.C. Nichols — kept many of the movement's ideals alive in Kansas City. His ideas meshed with Kessler's, who believed graceful boulevards, conforming to the city's topography, guaranteed the worth of bordering private property. As a realtor and developer, Nichols thought curving streets made interior property more valuable and helped create a community spirit.

Jesse Clyde Nichols, son of an Olathe grocer, came to Kansas City in 1905 after graduating from the University of Kansas and Harvard. He spent two years building speculative houses on strategic vacant lots in Kansas City, Kansas. He then purchased ten acres just south of the city limits (now about Fiftieth and Walnut streets), close to property William Rockhill Nelson was developing. As he began to lay out Countryside, his first subdivision, Nichols was influenced by Nelson's homebuilding philosophy and Kessler's planning.

He fused their ideas with principles of sound real estate development and park board ideas of aesthetics. Nichols understood how to finance beauty. "We must thank our park boards," he said, "for the inspiration to apply [aesthetics] to residential district development, but no idea is worthwhile unless it can in the long run pay its own way." Nichols imagined that home-owners would be willing to pay for the privilege of living in a beautiful environment. And he was right.

F.L. Olmsted, who believed subdivisions improved city life, also may have influenced Nichols. Olmsted was skeptical that crowded, dirty cities could ever be fashioned into quality places for living. His development of the Chicago suburb of Riverside, for instance, supported his idea that life is better if lived a little apart from the city.

Almost all of Nichols' early developments were beyond the city limits of Kansas City at that time. But he believed, as Olmsted did, that curving boulevards should connect his subdivisions with the city. In 1910, Nichols deeded ninety acres to the park board for Ward Parkway, a heartline boulevard in southwest Kansas City, that would link the city to his suburban developments, especially Mission Hills, at that time planned to be on both sides of State Line.

After receiving the right-of-way from Wornall Road to Gregory Boulevard, the board began to develop a beautiful parkway, landscaped with trees, gardens and priceless statuary, selected, purchased and placed by J.C. Nichols. Nichols brought columns, benches and urns. He brought statues from Italy to adorn the fountain at Meyer Circle, and in 1925, he purchased a magnificent eagle which had stood in the courtyard of a Japanese temple. He donated it to the city to place at Sixty-seventh and Ward Parkway.

The gift of a substantial length of Ward Parkway was the beginning of a unique, almost symbiotic relationship between the park board and the Nichols Company. Many areas of the city have benefited from this liaison but none more than the Country Club Plaza. As early as 1912, Nichols began to acquire land for the Plaza which he envisioned as the country's first shopping district designed for automobile drivers, not trolley riders. Before he could begin drawing plans, however, he had to buy the lime kiln of Lyle's Brickyard at Forty-ninth and Main Streets which daily put out enough black smoke to cover the entire Brush Creek Valley. Most of the rest of the land purchased for the Plaza was equally unappealing.

In 1913, when he was ready to lay out the area, Nichols created a stellar collaboration. He hired the landscape architecture firm of Hare & Hare on the recommendation of F.L. Olmsted, Jr., then in charge of the Boston firm founded by his father. Olmsted, Jr. had been one of Herbert Hare's professors at Harvard University, when young Hare was one of the first students in the Harvard architecture school's new city planning program.

Nichols also asked Kessler and Edward Delk to contribute to the design of the Plaza. They all agreed on a Spanish style of architecture, partly because of the area's historic trade with the Spanish of the southwest along the Santa Fe Trail, and partly because Nichols had loved Spain when he traveled there. Nichols completed the Plaza's first structure, the Suydam Building (now the Millcreek Building) in

(above) Penn Valley Park offers great variety of landscape in the center of the city. The first park board recognized the aesthetic potential of the area and acquired land for a large park with miles of pleasure drives within sight of downtown.

(right) The Scout has watched over a growing metropolis since his installation in 1922. The Cyrus Dallin statue so captured the imagination of the city on a touring visit here after the Pacific Exposition of 1915, that citizens raised $15,000 to purchase it.

The roads of Roanoke Park just south of Penn Valley Park wind into and out of beautiful natural scenery.

(above) By 1910, West Terrace Park was well-established and the West Bluff's rougher days nearly forgotten. The Tenth Street Outlook, shown here, today survives as almost the last remnant of this handsome park.

(above left) In the early decades of the 20th century, horse drawn oiling wagons, such as this one photographed in 1922, were a mainstay of boulevard maintenance.

(left) Swope Park's Music Pavilion has been used for all kinds of open air activities, including a barbecue dinner for the American Institute of Park Executives in September 1923.

Kansas City's bold initiatives in landscape design attracted national attention. The Mississippi Valley Chapter of the American Society of Landscape Architects met here in 1927 and looked over plans for the Liberty Memorial plaza. Sid Hare is fourth from the right.

George Kessler planted American elms in three staggered rows along Gladstone Boulevard at the turn of the century. Though some of these trees survived the Dutch Elm disease, pin oaks in a single row between the sidewalk and curb have been planted since 1964 as replacements.

In the early 1920s, Ward Parkway (shown here at Fifty-fifth Street) was the province of estate-sized properties, mansions, and elaborate formal gardens in the parkway itself.

1922, setting an architectural tone synonymous with beauty, symmetry and good taste and repeated in all his other Plaza buildings.

Herbert Hare had come back to Kansas City in 1910 to join his father Sidney J. Hare, who had established his firm in 1902. Sid Hare had come to Kansas City on a riverboat in 1868, and had studied horticulture, engineering, surveying, photography and geology before going to work in the city engineer's office in 1885. He worked there until 1896, during the time when the parks and boulevards were planned by Kessler, who became a mentor to Sid Hare. From 1896 to 1902, Hare weathered a local economic recession as superintendent of Forest Hill Cemetery. After he founded his firm, Hare developed a national reputation for park cemetery work, residential subdivisions, and institutional grounds.

He published widely, promoting the integration of rural qualities into urban designs, and the naturalistic massing of trees to increase the beauty and value of residential areas. These ideas suited Nichols' plans perfectly. In the combined ideas of the Hares, Kessler and Olmsted, Jr., he found exactly what he wanted for his Country Club District. Nichols' hiring of Hare & Hare moved the firm into a new level of planning opportunities. The intellectual collaboration and combined resources of Nichols, the park board, and Hare & Hare shaped Ward Parkway, the Country Club Plaza, the Municipal Rose Garden in Loose Park, and the grounds of the Nelson-Atkins Museum. Through these public spaces, the philosophy of the City Beautiful Movement was carried on in Kansas City and a lasting legacy of urban grace was defined.

From Battlefield to Urban Oasis

People of many beliefs settled the Kansas City area. Ideas about slavery were among the most passionately held of those beliefs and from the opening in 1862 of Kansas as a "free state" where slavery was outlawed, abolitionists and slave-holders violently opposed each other's beliefs. For several years before the Civil War was formally declared, violent border conflicts devastated the region and gave rise to the name "Bleeding Kansas." Missouri's border lands were ravaged, too. During the war, the bloodiest installment of the three-day Battle of Westport, sometimes called "The Gettysburg of the West," was fought on property that today is a peaceful park in the heart of the city.

Confederate soldiers under the command of General Sterling Price held the bluff south of Brush Creek, and Union forces were unable to dislodge them. Finally, a Union sympathizer showed the federal troops how to flank the Confederates by advancing up a draw west of a farm owned by trader William Bent. On October 23, 1864, Price's men, suffering heavy casualties, retreated across what is now Loose Park. Years later, Sunday strollers and picnickers often unearthed shot and other rusty reminders of the park's Civil War heritage.

In 1872, Seth Ward, a retired buffalo hunter and fur trader, purchased 400 acres of William Bent's farmland. He built a house on what is now Ward Parkway at Fifty-fifth Street and kept Bent's home intact behind it to use as a summer kitchen. Later, a Ward heir, Hugh Ward, and his wife were among the founders of the Kansas City Country Club, which leased the east pasture of the farm for one dollar a year and built a golf course and clubhouse here. Periodically, Ward's cows, still grazing in the west pasture, were beaned by errant golf balls.

In 1926, when the clubhouse burned and the Country Club purchased land further west, Hugh Ward's widow and her new husband, Ross Hill, former president of the University of Missouri, wanted to build low density houses on the former east pasture. However, J.C. Nichols, whose Countryside and Mission Hills residential developments were nearby, believed the loss of open space would lessen the quality of life in surrounding residential areas. He gave up on the hope that some Kansas City leaders held of Congress' appropriating money to set aside the land as a national park in honor of the Battle of Westport. Instead, he approached Mrs. Jacob L. Loose, widow of the chairman of the board of directors of the Loose-Wiles Biscuit Company, about buying the land for a park in memory of her husband, himself a notable local philanthropist, who had died in 1923.

In 1927, Mrs. Loose purchased the land for $500,000 and made a gift to the city of the property between Fifty-first and Fifty-fifth Streets, Wornall Road and Summit to be used as a park. Her conditions were that the park be used as a restful retreat, not as a recreational area for active sports such as golf or baseball, and that automobile traffic be restricted to a parking area near the entrance off Wornall Road. The city was also to remove the clubhouse on the land and replace it with a shelterhouse.

Twelve years later, Mrs. Loose donated more funds for the shelter house which was dedicated in October, 1939, on the seventy-fifth anniversary of the Battle of Westport. Sponsored by the Native Sons of Kansas City, the dedication also included placement of a red granite marker north of the Rose Garden in memory of the Grand Army of the Republic.

The Loose Park rose garden has delighted Kansas Citians from the time it was created in the early 1930s. In 1965, the board renamed the garden the Laura Conyers Smith Municipal Rose Garden, after the founder and first president of the Kansas City Rose Society. Mr. & Mrs. Kenneth Aber, among many others, have contributed significantly to the garden which was formally dedicated in 1938 and has been a mecca for flower lovers, a site for summer weddings, and a favorite stroll for people of all ages ever since. A fountain in the center of the garden was given to the city by the Florence and Oscar D. Nelson Fund and was dedicated in September 1980.

In 1978, the modern artist Christo gave Loose Park paths of gold when he wrapped the walkways in saffron colored nylon. The following January, Christo presented the board a scrapbook containing 449 articles and pictures of "Wrapped Walkways" which had appeared in 264 publications in the United States and abroad.

The original plan called for a conservatory and surrounding gardens which were never constructed, but in 1931, the city allotted an acre and half for a rose garden, sponsored by the Kansas City Rose Society. During the park's first decade, other gifts and further building helped create the character of the garden so beloved by Kansas Citians today. In 1935, the Kansas City Gardens Association gave a native stone lily pond to the garden and at the garden's dedication, Mrs. Massey Holmes presented the sculpted figure of a woman, *The Spirit of the Rose Garden*, to be placed along with fountain jets in the center of the pond in memory of her husband. It survived until sometime in the 1950s when it disappeared, probably taken by vandals. In 1980, a new, modern fountain was installed in the lily pond as a commemorative gift from the Oscar and Florence L. Nelson Fund. Oscar Nelson had been chairman of the board of Butler Manufacturing.

In 1939, a semi-circular stone pergola was built at the perimeter of the garden. Today climbing roses in elegant swags drape the walkway between the stone columns. In 1942, a Works Progress Administration project produced a wall fountain of larger-than-life-size figures of a man and a woman, installed in niches against a service building's south wall. Today the restored figures survive, but without the water effects.

The pond in Loose Park, now a special favorite of migrating ducks, small children, and radio-controlled boat owners, was an element of the original park. It was first enlarged as part of a federal relief project in 1934 and has been substantially enhanced over the years with stone and timber walls, terraced banks and a small island. A gift from the Junior League of Kansas City to celebrate the League's fiftieth anniversary allowed the lake to be rebuilt in 1964 and landscaped after the manner of a Japanese garden with a willow-shrouded bridge. In 1970, Mr. and Mrs. Richard Bloch's gift made possible the night lighting of the lagoon and surrounding area.

In addition to the rose garden, the pond, the shelter house, and the formal garden, the park's Stanley R. McLane Arboretum adds another dimension of pleasure with walkways and a running course beneath the trees. Altogether, Loose Park's facilities are attractive to hundreds of visitors each week and the park remains one of the most popular parks in the system. The effects of its steady use have concerned parks personnel and supporters, and volunteers have played important roles in nurturing Loose Park. Mrs. Moulton Green speaks for all Loose Park's committed protectors when she says, "So much of the history of our region and the beauty of our parks is exemplified by this place. All of us have a special duty to Loose Park."

In 1978, a unique artistic experiment took sedate, serene Loose Park out of its establishment mode, made it internationally famous for a brief period, and delighted almost everyone who saw it. The year-old Contemporary Art Society asked the park board to invite the artist Christo to Kansas City to wrap the walks of the park in saffron-colored nylon. Christo was an iconoclastic modern artist best known for his "Running Fence," a giant ribbon of nylon which ran for miles along the coast of California.

At first, the board was concerned about damage to the park and the safety of citizens walking on the cloth. To reassure them, Christo did a sample installation on a short section of walkway. After inspecting the sample, the board unanimously approved his request to wrap two-and-a-half miles of Loose Park's walks. Volunteers joined Christo's small staff to sew and lay down the hundreds of yards of fabric.

The project was a happy experience for those who helped install it. When they finished, the public had widely diverse comments along with the inevitable reference to the yellow brick road in the *Wizard of Oz*. A few thought the project was a total waste of time, money and effort. Others thought the walks were pretty and agreed with the *Kansas City Star's* comment that it "looked as if Rumpelstiltskin had spent the night spinning saffron nylon into gold." In the bright October sunlight, the walkways glistened like streets in a fairytale.

The park board and staff were delighted with the project and on October 24, the board passed a resolution commending Christo. Later, 15,140 square yards of material were distributed to interested schools, charities and churches or sold in a gala cutting party at the Starlight Theatre parking lot — one square yard to a person. The following January, Christo presented the board with a scrapbook containing 449 articles and pictures of "Wrapped Walkways" which had appeared within 264 publications in the United States and abroad.

Richard Marr, who was park board president at the time, said later, "People still remember and comment on it. Maybe it was out of character for Kansas City, way out of character — but it was fun! That's what parks are for."

*Built with funds from several bequests, especially from the estates of William Rockhill Nelson and Mary McAfee
Atkins, the Nelson-Atkins Museum of Art stands on the site of Nelson's home, Oak Hall. Its superb natural
setting has been enhanced by formidable design talents since the building was erected in 1933. Today it anchors
the cultural center of the city.*

CHAPTER IV

Riding Out the Depression

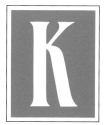ansas City weathered the tough years from 1930 to 1940 better than most American cities. Some observers credit a diversified economy. Others say Boss Tom Pendergast was able to bring more than the city's fair share of federal dollars this way. Everyone agrees that the pride and hopefulness of the citizens contributed a lot to easing the grip of hard times. Probably nothing illustrates the tenacious optimism of Kansas City more than the overwhelming vote supporting Kansas City's Ten Year bond program in 1931. William Allen White, the journalistic sage from Emporia, Kansas, termed the Ten Year Plan "Kansas City's monument to the Depression."

By any measure, it was the most comprehensive and ambitious civic undertaking since Kessler's 1893 Plan. The Ten Year program apportioned approximately $50 million (including $10 million in federal funds) for city and county improvements. The broad brush included a new city hall, courthouse, police building, Municipal Auditorium, water works system, and public market, as well as hospital additions and other important structures. New parks, playgrounds and boulevards, and improvements for existing park facilities also received funds.

However, the price of the successful bond election was the involvement of the city's political boss, Tom Pendergast, in spending the money and hiring construction workers. In the 1930s in Kansas City, Pendergast's Democratic machine dominated the city's political life. Those with the right politics were given patronage positions; 15,000 to 22,000 men with picks and shovels did work that half that many men using labor-saving tools could have done.

The voters approved $2,764,200 for park and boulevard improvements. Long-postponed work on the north approach to the Liberty Memorial, including the frieze on the north wall, received $887,000. The park board retained the Olmsted firm to prepare, design and superintend all aspects of Memorial Hill.

Citizens were disappointed, however, over the lack of other promised park improvements, particularly at the zoo. They questioned why certain bidders received contracts and jobs. When they learned that cement from Pendergast's Ready-Mixed Concrete Company paved Brush Creek, the outcry was especially long and loud. Many people complained the board spent too much bond money on boulevard resurfacing rather than for park improvements.

Regardless of the alleged waste, spectacular buildings, such as the now world-renowned Art Deco-style City Hall, Municipal Auditorium and Jackson County Courthouse remain a testament to the power of the city to raise funds and to the skills of marvelous craftsmen.

Pendergast's power in the Democratic Party increased when his candidate, Franklin Roosevelt, was elected in 1933. Already an important federal center since the establishment of the Federal Reserve bank here in 1914, Kansas City was an administrative hub for hundreds of New Deal programs, and the city benefited from many of these, particularly the Public Works and Works Progress Administration (WPA) which were especially interesting to Pendergast because of the opportunities to pave roads and use concrete. The WPA was responsible for extensive projects throughout the city and in the parks. Regardless of the propriety of payment for these projects, they produced a legacy of beautiful stonework and handsome buildings.

Parks were a source of employment for some during the Depression, but they were a source of enjoyment for tens of thousands of Kansas Citians, who, in addition to facing economic hardship, were also flattened during summer months by record heat waves in the 1930s. Before air-conditioning, whole families often spent the entire night in the parks, cooled somewhat by night breezes rustling through the trees. Citizens never appreciated the wonderful naturalness of their parks and parkways more.

Penn Valley was one of the most popular spots for park sleeping, and early morning travelers on Broadway or West Pennway were not surprised to see hillsides dotted with people sleeping as peacefully as if in their own beds.

W.H. Dunn, first superintendent of the Kansas City park system, guided the development of many of the city's premiere parks and boulevards, including beautiful Ward Parkway.

At Romany Road looking south in 1932, the trees newly planted along Ward Parkway were only a promise of the leafy beauty that shelters the thoroughfares today.

Soon after it was paved with concrete from Boss Tom Pendergast's Ready-Mixed Concrete Company, Brush Creek cut a broad, sparkling path beside the Country Club Plaza, seen here in 1932 from the roof of the Thomas Carlyle Hotel at Ward Parkway and Jefferson Street.

Almost all of Gillham Road could be considered a linear park. The topographically interesting land on either side of the thoroughfare has been developed by the park board into parks and playgrounds.

To divert runoff water from higher ground in Penn Valley, George Kessler built a system of underground drains and an earth dam which created a pretty lake in the northwest section of the park.

A beautiful new outdoor swimming pool was built at Swope Park in 1940 by men working for the Depression-era Works Progress Administration. Funding for the project came principally from the federal government's New Deal which provided hundreds of other projects that kept Kansas City's economy going during those hard years.

Many years elapsed between the building of the Liberty Memorial and the finishing of the north face of the monument and the landscaping of the grounds. The Great Frieze on the north of the memorial, facing Union Station, was finally completed in the 1930s by Edmond Amateis. The hill opposite Union Station leading up to the Liberty Memorial tested the patience of several park boards before it was eventually graded and landscaped.

Park Commissioner Ollie Gates reminisced: "I was born and raised on West Pennway, a beautiful area. The park department maintained it well. I remember many nights sleeping out in a triangle park at Eighteenth and Pennway and being awakened in the morning by a man cutting the grass with a long sickle, about to chop my legs off. All our neighborhood activities took place in that park, right there in front of my house. Parks made a big difference in my life."

Commissioner Carl DiCapo was born a block from Cliff Drive. "In the 1930s," he recalled, "we had no fans, nothing. My father used to take the family to the park, and we would sleep there. The neighbors would do the same. Those cool cliff breezes kept us comfortable all night."

In addition to sleeping, people gathered in the parks for free concerts, for games, for a sustaining spirit of community to ward off the emotional drain of economic problems. Perhaps at no other time in the city's life have the parks so clearly fulfilled their planners' vision, in which natural surroundings would help soothe the woes of humankind.

Kansas City had a national reputation as a "sin city" in the 1930s. Indeed, it was a hot town for nightlife, a cool town for jazz, and a wide-open town for liquor, prostitution, and gambling. But the parks represented a different Kansas City, one that seldom is described in the same breath with the jumpin' jazz legends. The parks were the quiet side: places where residents could lie down to sleep unharmed and could rise to see the earth's promise renewed, the blessing of morning sunlight on green trees. The New Deal fed the local economy, but the parks fed the local spirit.

During the years of the Depression, record heat waves and the need for inexpensive entertainment brought people to the parks. Boats on the Swope Park Lagoon raised a little breeze and a lot of high spirits.

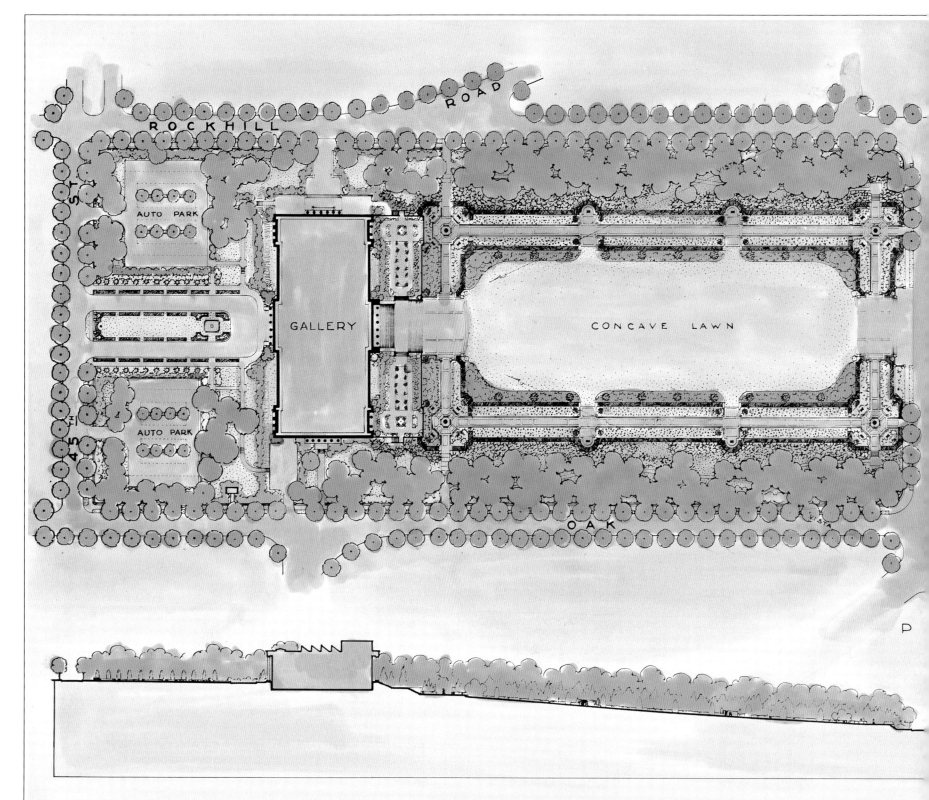

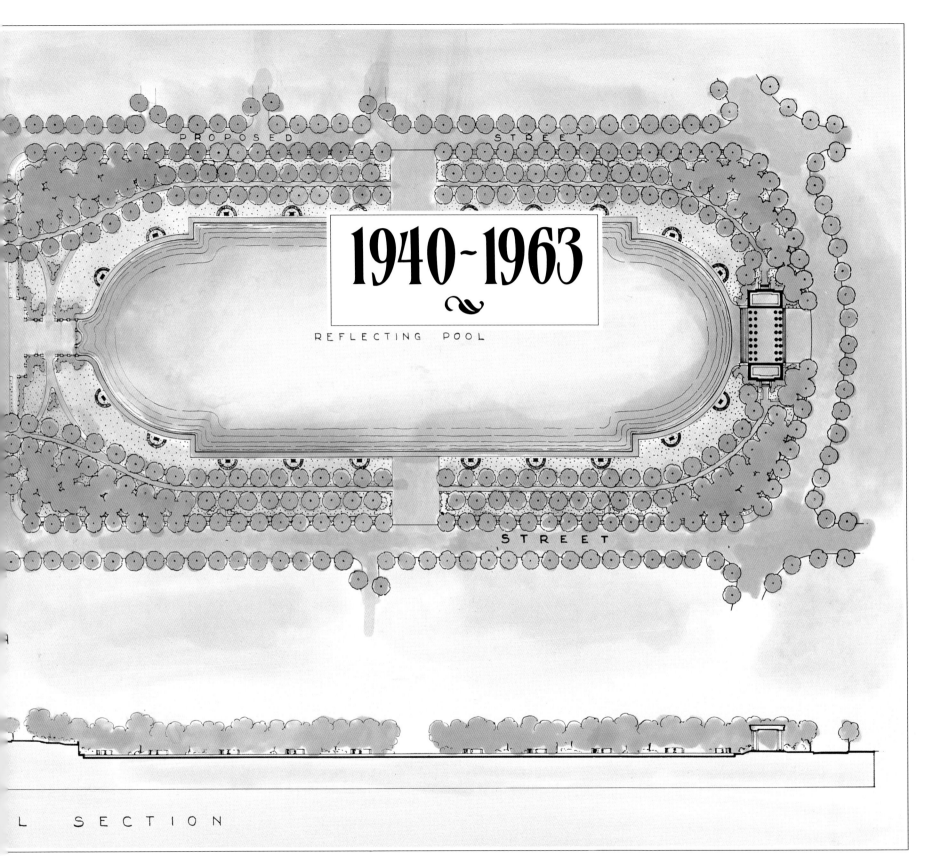

1940~1963

REFLECTING POOL

PROPOSED STREET

STREET

SECTION

Proposed General Plan of Grounds for William Rockhill Nelson Gallery of Art and Atkins Museum of Fine Arts

The J.C. Nichols Fountain is an appropriate introduction to the elegance of the Country Club Plaza, begun by Nichols in 1922 and continuously improved and beautified since.

CHAPTER V

A Changing Kansas City

hile Kansas City weathered the 1930s reasonably well, Boss Tom Pendergast did not. Excessive election irregularities spurred reformers who intensified their efforts to dismantle the machine, but before they could bring the Boss down, he was felled by gambling, bad health, and the Internal Revenue Service. In 1939, he went to jail for income tax evasion; he served fifteen months, returned home, and died in 1945. Reformers swept the city elections in 1940.

That year, L.P. Cookingham, a creative young city manager from Saginaw, Michigan, accepted Mayor John Gage's challenge to help rebuild citizen trust in Kansas City's government. When he arrived to assume the duties of city manager, Cookingham found a dispirited and divided city, ashamed of its past, more than $20 million in debt, but trying to make a new start under a reform mayor and council.

He also found a beautiful city, with remarkable parks and sweeping boulevards. Although as city manager he did not officially work with the park board, Cookingham often attended board meetings. "I got along just as well with members of the park board as if I had appointed them myself," he recalled, "and I never had any criticism of what they were doing or what they were not doing."

Some other people *were* critical, saying the parks were suffering aesthetically. The new park board, appointed by Mayor Gage, decided it needed a trained consultant, an expert on landscape architecture, to assure proper scale and harmony in the parks and along the boulevards.

The board retained S. Herbert Hare of Hare & Hare. Hare had served as a consultant to the board for two years after Kessler's death, in 1923, but that board abolished his position in 1930, reportedly because the Pendergast Democratic machine thought Hare did not perform politically. Although the park board was nonpartisan, during the Pendergast years the political machine influenced much of its activity.

One board member appointed by Gage in 1940 was Edwin R. Chandler of Chandler Landscape and Floral Company. He was especially suited to serve because as a boy he had gone on inspection tours in a horse and buggy with his father, the district park superintendent. Kessler became acquainted with the elder Chandler when the two worked on the St. Louis World's Fair in 1904, and Kessler brought him to Kansas City.

Even after the reform government was in place, residual effects of boss rule lingered. In 1941, Commissioner Chandler, a Republican, called for a probe of political activity within the park department. A report by the city auditor charged the United Democratic Club with soliciting membership among park employees, contrary to the letter and spirit of the city charter. The board asked two employees to resign but cleared and reinstated a third man.

No one could deny the pervasiveness of Pendergast, but the new park board worked to eliminate partisanship. The board required the city personnel department to establish qualifications for park department performance and to prepare exams to reveal those qualifications. During its first year in office, the board accepted the resignations of 242 park employees, reducing the number working for the department by fifty percent. The park department was beginning to heal the wounds inflicted by machine politics.

In 1941, the conflict in Europe began to influence the actions of Kansas City officials. The park board, as well as other governmental units still trying to effect reform, set aside other concerns and prepared for possible involvement in a World War.

In July before the attack on Pearl Harbor, the park board leased an area west of Wyandotte between Twenty-ninth and Thirtieth Streets to the War Department for three years at one dollar per year, to be used for an Army recreation camp. In September, the board gave the War Department the same terms for five acres on part of the Parade on The Paseo for military recreation. In 1944, the government was released from both leases. In April 1945, the board received a request for approval for the Penn Valley camp to be used by the

A ride around the Swope Park lagoon on the "Clipper" was a delightful warm weather excursion during the 1940s.

Big Jim Pendergast, First Ward Alderman, saloon owner and powerful political influence in Kansas City during the early years of the 20th century, was an early friend of the fledgling parks and boulevard movement. Grateful for his help, the park board in 1913 dedicated this bronze statue which was placed in Mulkey Square. In 1990, the board refurbished the monument, placed it at Clark Point at 8th and Jefferson Street and rededicated it.

Band concerts and sing-alongs in Loose Park were popular summertime activities during the 1930s and 1940s.

STARLIGHT THEATRE SHINES AGAIN

The "almost completed" Starlight Theatre welcoming Kansas City's second century made such a great impression on the public that the Starlight Theatre Association was born under the leadership of former Park Board President John A. Moore who became the first Starlight Theatre Association President. On June 25, 1951, more than 6,000 theatergoers attended the first musical, "A Desert Song."

For more than three decades, Kansas City families enjoyed the musical theater and rated the Starlight Theatre a top summertime activity. But in the 1980s, changing tastes in entertainment, poorly received shows, and bad summer weather combined to drop attendance, and the Starlight Theatre Association found itself in serious financial trouble.

A group of civic leaders working with Jack Steadman, president of the association, began to turn things around. The group included Woody Bennett, John Ayres, Ernest Dick and Robert Kipp.

In 1987, Mrs. Clyde Nichols was named ticket chairman and the Kansas City Star carried an article with the headline "Can Nichols Save the Starlight?" Suddenly aware that the outdoor theater was in genuine danger, Kansas City responded. People bought tickets and came to shows. The hard work of dedicated volunteers and staff took the association from an indebtedness of $500,000 to a profit within two years.

"During the first winter, the park department kept us alive by paying for staff," Mrs. Nichols recalled.

Today the theater is firmly reestablished and is once again one of Kansas City's best-loved summer entertainments.

Starlight Theater opened May 25, 1950 in time for the city's centennial birthday pageant and has been a civic institution ever since. The theater has enjoyed a revitalization of interest and is a thriving summertime entertainment.

government again, this time for a prisoner of war camp, but the board denied the request because of adverse public reaction.

Shortly after war was declared, the board carved out an area on the north side of Meyer Boulevard, east of Troost Avenue, for victory gardens. A tractor and driver were supplied at $1.50 an hour for use by gardeners.

The board also endorsed the planting of trees on the east side of Liberty Memorial Mall by Navy War Mothers as living memorials to their sons, with the west side of the mall to be used by the Army Mothers Club. In November, 1945, additional trees were planted by the Army Mothers Club in a memorial ceremony for the dead of both World Wars. As a result, the Liberty Memorial Mall now boasts an avenue of trees.

In 1942, the Kansas City chapter of the American War Mothers paid for a commemorative shrine saluting the enduring service to country of both mothers and sons. An obelisk with jets of water spraying from each side into a ceramic tile pool at its base was designed by Kansas City architect Edward Buehler Delk for the memorial, which is located at Meyer Boulevard and The Paseo.

With these exceptions, park board activity from 1941 to 1945 almost stopped. But as the war began to wind down, the board began discussing postwar plans. Construction of an outdoor theater at Swope Park that could seat 7,500 people was given the highest priority. In 1944 the board asked Edward Delk to design a Starlight Theatre that would rival any open air theater in the country.

Kansas Citians had long dreamed of an outdoor theater. A benefit musical program staged at the American Royal Building in November 1926 for Queen Marie of Rumania had netted $7,000. Participants and promoters had wanted this money earmarked for an outdoor theater on the grounds of the Kansas City Art Institute. But neighbors' objections had effectively killed that plan.

Then, in 1947, citizens approved a $44 million bond program, including $500,000 for an outdoor theater. The park board and Delk chose the Swope Park site, and construction began in December 1949. More than 150 workmen raced to finish the structure in time for Kansas City's 100th birthday celebration pageant, "Thrills of a Century," scheduled for May 25, 1950. Despite frigid winter weather, the men lost only five working days, and the pageant opened on time.

By 1955, the avenue of trees planted by the Navy War Mothers and the Army Mothers Club as memorials to their sons were an impressive element of the Liberty Memorial Mall.

Sculptor Richard Hunt was inspired by the flaming forces of freedom and the fluidity of jazz music when he created the sculpture for the fountain, located at Brush Creek Boulevard and Cleveland Avenue. It was dedicated on the anniversary of the death of Bruce R. Watkins, a black civic and political leader who worked tirelessly to create support for the project. The Spirit of Freedom Fountain represents the contributions of black citizens to Kansas City.

CHAPTER VI

The City of Fountains

idway through the twentieth century, Kansas City lost two men who had been powerful shapers of the community's life. William Volker, businessman and philanthropist, died in 1947 and J.C. Nichols, visionary real estate developer, died in 1950.

Although neither served on the park board, their civic activities supported the ideal behind the parks and boulevards, the ideal of a city where residents could live their lives to the fullest. Many people wanted to honor these leaders and the park board responded by locating memorial fountains in areas of the city associated with each man's good works.

These two fountains stimulated a renewed interest in public fountains. Kansas City's many streams and the springs trickling from limestone formations had made running water a part of the town's landscape from the beginning. The first fountains were simple and served a purpose: they provided drinking water for man and beast. Public drinking troughs were built throughout the late nineteenth century but the first really "hygienic" fountain, designed through its overflow and drainage system to prevent the spread of disease, was dedicated in 1910 to honor Frank Faxon, a former president of the Humane Society. Some other fountains of similar design and use were built, and private fountains were put in private parks or used to ornament homes and commercial buildings, but many were soon dry, victims of technical difficulties, sanitary objections, or simple lack of maintenance. Even Kessler's 1893 plan contained mention of only two specific fountains, one on The Paseo and one in West Terrace Park.

Not until J.C. Nichols began his residential communities were fountains a significant part of the landscape. Fascinated with both fountains and statuary and with rustic, natural water elements, in the early 1920s, he began buying fountains and other art to beautify his residential developments and to enhance the Country Club Plaza. Splashing water became a Nichols trademark.

Along Ward Parkway, fountains and pools are a refreshing recollection of his foresight in planning watery solutions to the increasing encroachment of concrete and asphalt into city life. The Sea Horse Fountain at Meyer Circle on Ward Parkway is one of the best examples of Nichols' blend of water and wonderful statuary. In 1924, when the park board was developing the Meyer Circle, Nichols proposed a fountain using seventeenth century Venetian cherubim and seahorse figures he had purchased on a trip to Italy earlier in the decade. Nichols installed the fountain and pool, designed by Edward Buehler Delk, and asked the park board to take responsibility for landscaping and upkeep.

Since the mid-1960s, with the increase in volume and speed of automobile traffic, Meyer Circle has been the site of numerous accidents with resulting proposals to straighten the trafficway and move the fountain. These meet with steady resistance; the people of Kansas City are passionate about protecting the works of art and the beloved sites that give the city its special character. Although the controversy continues, the late Carl Migliazzo, former park commissioner, may have summed up the public's feeling when he said that if the transportation department "wants to continue turning boulevards into trafficways, they should melt down the *Pioneer Mother* sculpture in Penn Valley Park and recast it as a monument to the automobile."

William Volker was a more private public figure than Nichols. Volker's civic contributions were most often made directly to Kansas City's needy. A quietly charitable person whose window shade business made him a millionaire by 1906, he kept fragmentary records of his good deeds and deservedly earned the nickname, "Mr. Anonymous."

However, he was a dynamic leader when it came to the important work of the city's Welfare Department, which he helped institute. He served fourteen years on the Kansas City School Board and was adamant about the need for an institution of higher education in the center of the city for urban youth who must work and study at the same time.

The theme of Volker's fountain is based on the life of St. Martin

Contributions from Kansas City school children were among the many private gifts that provided the magnificent equestrian fountain at Mill Creek Park honoring J.C. Nichols, whose residential developments kept the City Beautiful tradition alive in Kansas City.

of Tours, a French patron saint who split his coat in half to share it with a beggar on a bitterly cold evening. Later Christ appeared in the saint's dream wearing the coat, according to the legend. In comparing Martin of Tours to William Volker, the Swedish sculptor, Carl Milles, evoked the profound respect each had for the dignity of every man.

Milles worked closely with the park board, architect Edward Buehler Delk and landscape architect S. Herbert Hare to choose the site for the fountain, anchoring what was envisioned to be a great cultural mall linking the Nelson-Atkins Museum of Art with the University of Kansas City (now the University of Missouri-Kansas City). The fountain project was delayed by problems of funding and land acquisition. It was already two years behind its scheduled 1953 completion when Milles died in 1955. Then Delk died in 1956. Architect Edward Tanner, who was a member of the Volker Memorial Committee, continued the planning, and the fountain was dedicated in September, 1958.

No other single fountain in Kansas City is emblematic of so much of the city's cultural and civic life at once. The long-imagined cultural mall is not yet a complete reality, but today the fountain in the Brush Creek valley, not far from the Volker campus of the university which he was so instrumental in establishing, celebrates Volker, as well as Frank Theis, park board president for whom the park is named, sculptor Milles, architects Delk and Tanner and landscape architect Hare.

Although, in a sense, many fountains memorialize J.C. Nichols, a special fountain seemed the most fitting tribute to him. In 1952, the family purchased an equestrian grouping originally sculpted in 1910 in Paris by Henri Greber, designed for a fountain on the Long Island estate of Clarence Mackay. In 1957, the park board adopted a resolution to construct a Nichols memorial fountain on park lands and recommended a site on the north side of Forty-seventh Street between J.C. Nichols Parkway and Main Street.

Miller Nichols, son of the developer, offered the Greber sculpture, then appraised at $250,000. The park board pledged $5,000 a year over five years to pay part of the construction costs. The rest of the $125,000 installation cost was raised through private contributions, including gifts from Kansas City school children. Missing parts of the fountain group were created by Kansas City sculptor Herman Frederick Simon, who had crafted the bronze doors of the Kansas City City Hall and the Jackson County Courthouse, and architect Edward Tanner designed the fountain itself. The fountain was dedicated in May 1960.

After these two fountains were installed, interest in fountains gained momentum. In the Downtown area, redevelopment plans were changing the urban center, but commercial interests had superseded beautification. A fountain would make a welcome addition. When construction began on the Commerce Tower Building at 911 Main, James M. Kemper, Sr. began to work toward the monument he had long envisioned as a memorial to his son, Lt. David Woods Kemper, who was killed in World War II. He commissioned New York sculptor Wheeler Williams to create a fountain representing the spirit of the Missouri River.

Williams created a beautiful bronze goddess, the Muse of the Missouri, holding a net from which fish are spilling. Two hundred bursts of water form pools in three basins at the base of the fountain. The board dedicated The Muse in 1963 and placed her on Main Street between Eighth and Ninth Streets.

In the mid-1960s, when New York's Pennsylvania Station was razed, the Boy Scouts in Kansas City requested and received from the railroad the sculpture pieces which had been over the Seventh Avenue entrance to the station. The group consists of two women, representing day and night, standing on either side of a huge wreath. When the board placed the pieces at Thirty-ninth Street and Gillham Road, Kansas City architect Maurice McMullen designed a setting including a fountain cascading into a reflecting pool flanked by two spiral concrete stairways. He added a Boy Scout Eagle badge to the wreath's center. The finished monument, a gift of Mr. and Mrs. John W. Starr, was dedicated in 1968 to Eagle Scouts nationwide.

In 1973, a group organized by Harold Rice, a Hallmark Cards vice president, outlined a proposal to the park board for a "City of Fountains Foundation." The board enthusiastically adopted his idea to solicit money for a trust fund that would build a fountain each year in Kansas City and provide maintenance. Since then, eleven fountains in all sections of the metropolitan area have been constructed and dedicated and more are planned.

The first was Heritage Fountain dedicated October 5, 1977, a stately pylon 400 feet above the banks of the Blue River in Blue Valley Park. Its magnificent sprays of water can be seen for miles.

The Spirit of Freedom Fountain, at Brush Creek Boulevard and Cleveland Avenue, was dedicated September 13, 1981, one year after the death of Bruce R. Watkins, a prominent civic leader and park board member. Watkins had worked tirelessly for a fountain that would symbolize the heritage and contributions of Kansas City's black community and serve as a dramatic introduction to the city from the southeast.

The sculptor Richard Hunt, inspired by the fiery nature of

Dedicated to the memory of William Volker, this fountain in Theis Park was created by Carl Milles and is based on the life of St. Martin of Tours, one of France's patron saints. The park board accepted it as a fitting tribute to Volker's seemingly limitless compassion and generosity.

Sculpture pieces rescued from the razed Pennsylvania Station in New York City were used by Kansas City architect Maurice McMullen to create a monument that honors Eagle Scouts nationwide. A gift from Mr. and Mrs. John W. Starr, the memorial is located at Thirty-ninth Street and Gillham Road.

The first fountain north of the Missouri River at North Oak Street and North Vivion Road is now a centerpiece of the lovely park area recently named the Anita B. Gorman Park in honor of the Northlander who served on the park board for twelve years.

*Built in 1925, the Sea Horse Fountain — better known as the Meyer Circle Fountain on Ward Parkway —
symbolizes Kansas City's dedication to priceless beauty. The figures in the fountain were bought by J.C. Nichols
in Italy where they had stood for 300 years in a Venetian square.*

freedom and the free form of Kansas City jazz, created a piece featuring modernistic bronze projections that curve skyward from a gray granite pedestal. A reflecting pool surrounding the base of the sculpture spouts jets of water toward the flame-like symbols of freedom.

The Northland fountain, the first fountain north of the river, was the result of years of work by Northland residents. So much public effort was directed at the project that some people said it should be called "the People's Fountain." Designed by architect Homer Williams, it was dedicated June 21, 1983, in the forty-one-acre Anita B. Gorman Park on the southeast corner of North Oak Trafficway and Vivion Road. The Northland fountain received an Urban Design Award from the Municipal Art Commission in 1984.

Other fountains built and maintained by the City of Fountains Foundation include the fountain in Spring Valley park, dedicated to the memory of civic leader Bernard Powell; the Columbus Square fountain; the Robert Gillham fountain; the 49-63 neighborhood fountain at Lydia Street and The Paseo; and the Vietnam Veterans Fountain at Forty-third and Broadway.

Garment District Place, a brick plaza in the garment district at Eighth and Broadway, is the site of a fountain built with funds provided by the Godfrey and Blanche Jones Memorial Trust and the Procter and Gamble Co. and dedicated in July, 1991. Plans are underway to build a children's fountain in the Northland; a major gateway fountain at Sixth and Admiral; and a major ornamental fountain near Twelfth and Vine Streets, the spiritual and historic home of Kansas City jazz. The Firefighters' Fountain in Penn Valley Park is nearing completion.

In addition to building new fountains, the park board wanted to restore the city's valuable bronze statues and fountain sculptures, badly damaged over the years by air pollution. In September 1984, the board heard a report by R.F. Corwin on the severely deteriorated condition of the Pioneer Mother and the Volker fountain sculpture group. Once thought to be indestructible, the pieces were being damaged by toxic car fumes and other air pollutants. In 1986, the Volker fountain pieces were restored, followed by work on the J.C. Nichols fountain and the Pioneer Mother.

In June 1986, the board entered into an agreement with the Greater Kansas City Community Foundation and Affiliated Trusts to establish an Outdoor Bronze Restoration Fund. The board was concerned also about the structural conditions of the city's fountains, many eroded by age and plagued with serious electrical problems. Park board members Carl DiCapo, Ollie Gates and Anita Gorman approached Robert J. Reeds, manager of city and county affairs for the Kansas City Power & Light Company, and asked if the utility company would be willing to become involved in solving the electrical problems and upgrading the conditions around the fountains. After consultation with Drue Jennings, KCP&L chief executive officer, Reeds told the board, yes. He went even further and proposed an "Adopt a Fountain" program, which the board adopted in 1989, to insure complete and continuing upkeep for the city's priceless fountains.

Since then, several groups have assumed responsibility for restoring particular fountains. The Kansas City Metro Medical Society has raised funds to restore the William Fitzsimmons Memorial at Twelfth Street and The Paseo, and the Central Exchange is sponsoring the renovation of the fountain at Ninth Street and The Paseo, which they have named the Women's Leadership Fountain. By 1990, more than half a million dollars had been spent on restoring twelve major outdoor bronze pieces with an additional twenty-four reported in need of care.

Among the most significant community partnerships are the joint efforts of the park board, The City of Fountains Foundation and the "Adopt-a-Fountain" program. Their shared guardianship of the city's fountains assures the continued beauty and pleasure provided by these Kansas City treasures.

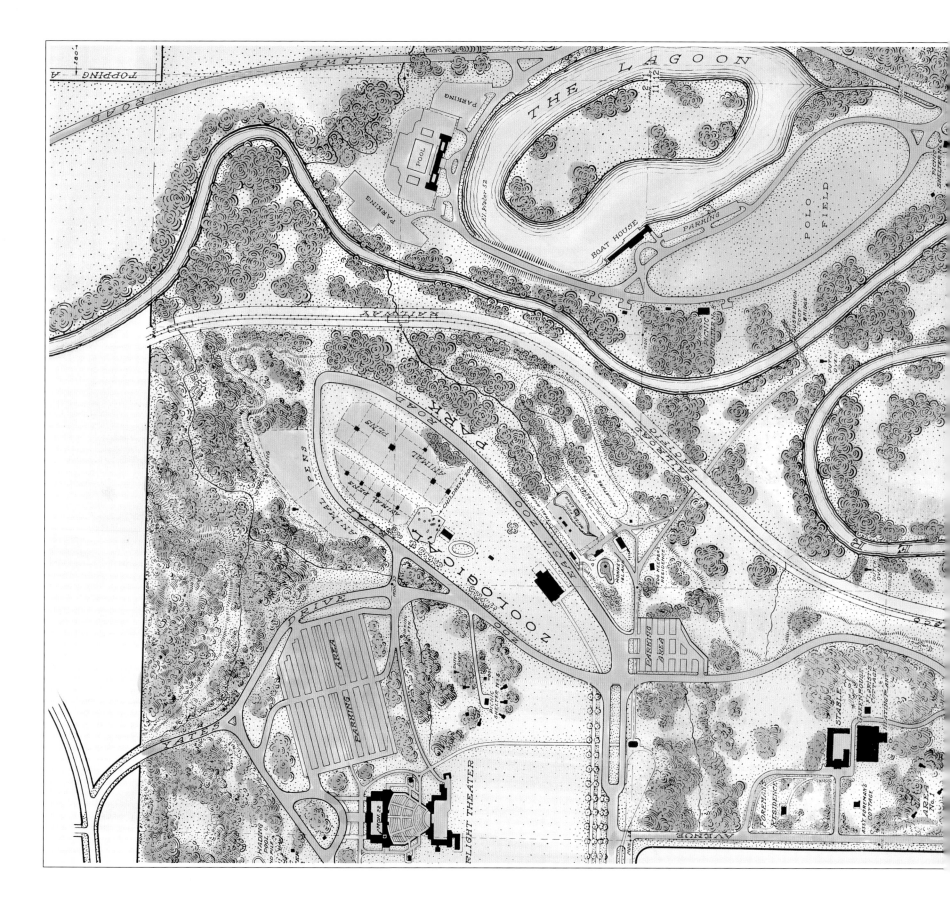

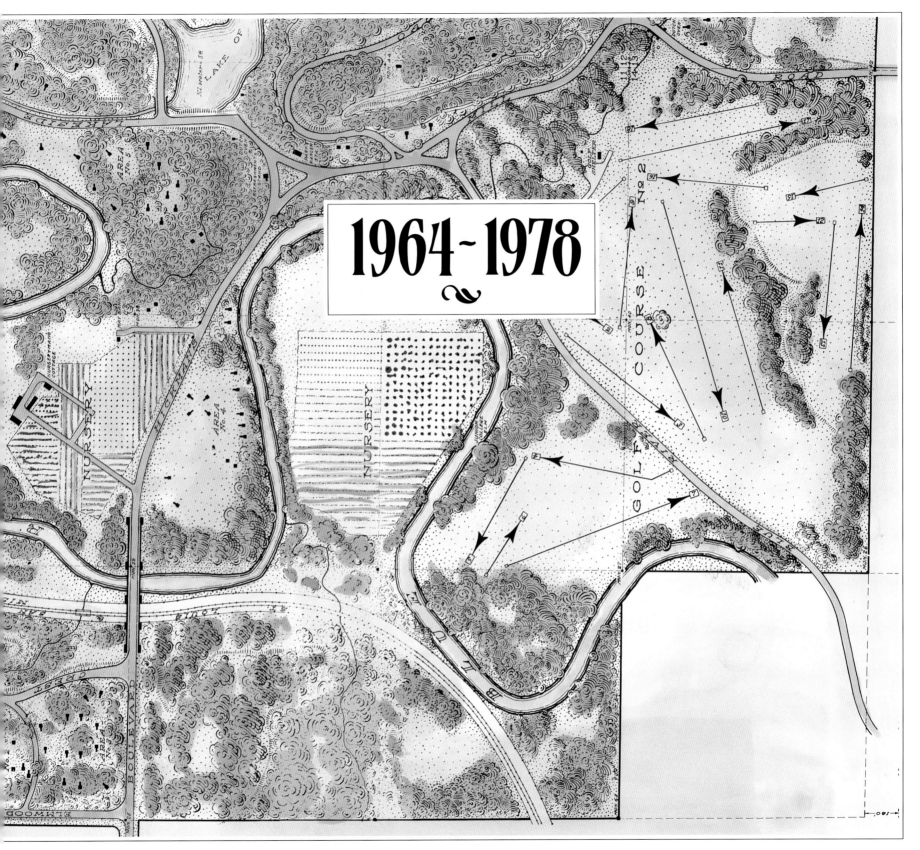

1964~1978

Early Map of Swope Park.

Chromatic reflectors created as a Solar Field by Kansas City sculptor Dale Eldred play with the sunlight and the imagination of pedestrians and motorists along Brush Creek Boulevard during the summer of 1979.

CHAPTER VII

Leadership for a New Era

n a retrospective of a hundred years of park board achievements, certain years are clearly pivotal. The post-war recovery and the decade of the 1950s were years of stabilization in Kansas City and the parks reflected this with a period of more maintenance than growth. It was also a time when Americans' lifestyles changed significantly: television sets and air-conditioning kept people home after work. Family outings in the park became occasional events rather than regular activities. For many families, the automobile became an important part of leisure: the Sunday drive replaced a stroll in the park.

By the early 1960s patterns like these had contributed to weakening the parks system. Additionally, the city had been struggling financially to recover from Pendergast and the war, as well as to create an infrastructure to support modern urban life. Parks funding wasn't a priority.

According to former mayor Ilus Davis, the system was "suffering from malnourishment." After more than twenty-four years as park superintendent, J.V. Lewis was leaving the post. Only the second superintendent to serve the park board, Lewis became superintendent in February 1939 after the retirement of W.H. Dunn. He served through the last years of the Depression, through the Pendergast regime, and into the years of World War II and its aftermath. By December 1963, he was ready to retire.

Frank Theis, president of the board, knew of Frank Vaydik, a top administrator in the Detroit parks system, and believed he was the man to turn things around in Kansas City. When they met with Vaydik at a national convention of park administrators in 1963, Theis and his fellow commissioners, Dr. Robert Hodge and Lewis Dysart, offered Vaydik the job, but he turned them down.

"I told them, 'I don't think I'm interested at all, but I'll consider it'," Vaydik said. "I didn't know much about Kansas City, although they did have a bad reputation in that they had no money and were not getting things done. They'd had a fine reputation for years, but it had been going down hill. I went home and within a week or two, I got a call from Frank Theis. I said, 'I'm not really interested' and that ended the conversation. He called a few days later. This kept up all fall. I began to almost believe him that I could make a difference in Kansas City." After a trip to Kansas City and more phone calls from Theis, Vaydik finally agreed to accept the challenge.

During his sixteen years in Kansas City, Vaydik enhanced the park system, doubling its size, developing parkland north of the river, acquiring new land and improving already developed land south of the river. He also merged recreation with parks and stimulated new programs to bring people back to using the parks. Unfortunately, Theis did not live to see what his insistence on professionalism meant for the future of the system. He died in November 1965, only a year after Vaydik became director.

A quiet, self-effacing man, Frank Theis was born in Kansas City in 1890 and earned a law degree at the University of Kansas. As a young man he worked in the Hastings, Nebraska, branch office of the Armour Grain Company which his father, John A. Theis, managed in Kansas City. He returned to Kansas City to join the Simonds, Shields, Lonsdale Grain Company (now Simonds, Shields and Theis) against the advice of his father, who thought he should set up a law practice.

Frank Theis became an important force in Kansas City because of his fine business reputation, his devotion to civic service and his humanitarianism. Though he served on many boards and for many causes, "the park board was his baby," says his son, Willis Theis, "and he loved it." During his time on the board, Frank Theis never publicly belabored park problems, but he worked diligently with civic leaders to achieve the changes he knew were needed, his son recalls.

One of his visions was a cultural center connecting the Nelson-Atkins Museum of Art and Midwest Research Institute, extending south to the University of Missouri-Kansas City, Rockhurst College and the Linda Hall Library. "He thought the whole thing together was a natural package," his son says.

Frank Theis imagined this area in a context of dramatic open

The park board and the community carefully deliberated a final decision on the location of the Westport Roanoke Community Center, shown here in the early 1960s. Eventually, the center was built on Roanoke Road in Roanoke Park which has proved to be an excellent site for access by the community this center serves.

One of the most popular golf courses in the city, the Minor Park course was designed and built by park employees on land given the city in 1956 by Marie Minor Sanborn in memory of her father, William E. Minor.

Park director Frank Vaydik received national press attention in 1964 when he reversed the sentiments of traditional "Keep Off the Grass" warnings with signs inviting the public to enjoy the parks by walking all over them.

space. During his tenure he cleared more than thirteen acres between Brush Creek and Volker Boulevards. The board purchased and razed twenty-four houses built by William Rockhill Nelson at the turn of the century just south of Nelson's own home on the present site of the Nelson Art Gallery. Frank Theis' first vote as a park board commissioner was for a resolution naming the road bisecting this cultural corridor after the great humanitarian, William Volker.

The park board named the open land the Frank A. Theis Memorial Mall a year after his death; in 1991 it was renamed Frank A. Theis Park as part of the beginning of extensive Brush Creek redevelopment. With these two memorials to Volker and Theis, the board linked together forever two of Kansas City's most far-sighted leaders.

∾

"Please Walk On The Grass"

When the board called on Frank Vaydik to confront Dutch Elm disease in 1962, he was not impressed that the city had tried to disguise the problem by spraying dead trees green.

"That didn't add up at all," Vaydik says. "They [the trees] should have been pulled out and not had any at all, rather than trying to fool people." He also was disillusioned about the way Kansas City had treated its heritage. He believed the city did not appreciate its parks and boulevards system and was not preserving it.

Vaydik had insisted he was not interested in the job, but when he visited Kansas City, "we showed him the land north of the river" Commissioner Lewis Dysart says, "and it was like showing a glutton a room full of food. He saw that he could do in the Northland what Kessler had done in his 1893 Plan" and he agreed to come.

It was a big move, Vaydik says, "but it was the finest thing that ever happened to me. It was refreshing to come to Kansas City because I had all the opportunity in the world."

"The first thing he called to our attention," says Dr. Robert Hodge, "was that we did not have a master plan as to how the system was to grow and in what dimensions. Working with staff planner Herb Brackney, Vaydik came up with a master plan for the famous boulevard system in Kansas City south. The plan also laid out the lines where this boulevard system would be north of the river and called for four major parks there to be connected by boulevards."

During the 1960s, under the presidency of Lyndon Johnson, the federal government offered millions of dollars to communities for local beautification projects and park facilities expansion. Frank Vaydik and Brackney were adept at designing grants and petitioning the government for funds. "We got one of the first—if not the first—grant in the nation," Vaydik says. "I knew a lot of people in Washington, and that helped."

Dr. Hodge recalls that the city also hired additional people with the federal money. "We ended up with a labor force as well as money available in matching funds," he says, "and, of course, we felt land would never again be as cheap in the north. It was time to buy it and lay it aside. Later we lost federal money. We pretty much got our land in place, but we had to hold back on development."

Vaydik's master plan called for almost doubling park and boulevard land from 5,800 acres to 10,500. To buy the land, he proposed selling $2,221,000 in park bond funds, which the voters had already authorized, and he asked for an additional $250,000 for development of land purchased.

Two hundred and twenty-seven acres at Holmes and Red Bridge Roads were already awaiting development. In 1956, Marie Minor Sanborn had donated the land to Kansas City in memory of her father, William E. Minor, and Vaydik thought it would be an ideal public golf course. He asked several well-known golf course planners to lay out a course, but they all wanted too much money.

"Finally," Ilus Davis remembers, "Vaydik realized he could not get a golf course built within the budget, so he took a group of park department employees, a bulldozer and a few odd machines and started to build a golf course he planned himself, then had professionally laid out by Larry Flatt. Within a few months, he had an operating golf course which today is heavily used and regarded as a great asset."

At one time, Vaydik had considered becoming a professional golfer. He had played golf and basketball at Michigan State University. As director of Kansas City's parks, he maintained the pace of an athlete in top condition. Soon, Kansas City realized a whirlwind was at work. Long-neglected parks and boulevards took on a new look. Staff repaired crumbling walks, mowed grass, removed dead trees, cut back overgrown brush, pulled weeds and repaired fountains. Then they turned those fountains on from Easter until the fall celebration of the American Royal instead of the brief Memorial Day-to-Labor Day summer season.

Vaydik recalls that during his first months here, he noticed how shabby the playground equipment looked. "So," he says, "I called my staff in and said, 'We're going to have a bee. We're going to paint

A young participant in the Line Creek Archeology Program digs in a demonstration site at Line Creek Park where Hopewell Indian artifacts have been discovered.

Following the retirement of Frank Vaydik (above) in 1980, the board named the Frank Vaydik Line Creek Park, honoring his outstanding work for the Kansas City park system.

The Northland's beautiful Hodge Park was named for Dr. Robert Hodge, affectionately known as "Mr. Park Board," who served on the board for twelve years, four of them as president.

this equipment. You make up your own color combinations. I don't care what you paint them — just paint them.' Then there was an editorial in the *Star* that said, 'Look at all the new equipment'! Well, we didn't put in one single piece of new equipment . . . we just made it visible to the public. They didn't realize what they had."

Vaydik made another highly visible change during those first months: he placed "Please Walk on the Grass" signs in all the parks "to encourage people to enjoy their parks as they should," he says. "We got some national press attention over that."

With his first federal grant, on the recommendation of archeologist Mette Shippie, Vaydik purchased Line Creek Park in Platte County, a 120-acre tract north of the river. The site of a village of mound-dwelling Hopewell Indians in about A.D. 900, the land was slated for development. In a dramatic rescue, Mayor Ilus Davis listened to the pleas of amateur and professional archeologists and historians and personally ordered the bulldozers off the property until a study could be made of its historic significance to the community. Soon after development was halted, the city bought the land.

The park features fenced areas for roaming buffalo and elk and exhibits of Indian culture. Following Vaydik's retirement in 1980, the board named the land Frank Vaydik Line Creek Park, honoring his outstanding work for the Kansas City park system.

Early in 1967, the board accepted 385 acres for a park along Shoal Creek in the Northland. Eventually it was expanded to 623 acres. After his retirement, the park commissioners named the park for Dr. Robert Hodge, known affectionately as "Mr. Park Board" because of his long and productive tenure on the board. The park has an eighteen-hole golf course, a small lake and other facilities, including Shoal Creek, Missouri, a collection of restored and reconstructed buildings built between 1820 and 1860.

The board acquired land for two other Northland parks during Vaydik's tenure: Hidden Valley Park at Russell Road and North Bennington; and Tiffany Springs Park, 385 acres just south of Kansas City International airport.

In 1975, the first parkway opened north of the river, the mile-long Searcy Creek Parkway. Vaydik calls the boulevard system "the great thing Kansas City has going for it. If it were not for the boulevards," he says, "Kansas City would be just another big urban area. The boulevards add character to the city. Paris is the only place I know of that is comparable."

As he closed his career in Kansas City, Vaydik received the top award in his field, the National Distinguished Professional Award

from the National Recreational and Park Association. He had returned a tarnished system to its former lustre and set in place an extension of that grandeur in the city north of the river.

A Canopy of Green

If Kansas City has a singular glory, it is trees. Perhaps nothing surprises visitors as much as the multitude and variety of the city's trees. The official Kansas City tree is the American elm.

Trees figured prominently in all the plans for the original and subsequent parks. J.C. Nichols took his cue from landscape planners and sometimes rerouted his streets to save special trees. He maintained company nurseries to provide trees to new home-buyers because he believed no home was complete without them.

By the mid-twentieth century, Kansas City's arboreal holdings were vast, and premier amongst these were the elms. For years, the elms' graceful and abundant foliage sheltered homes and thoroughfares from summer's oppressive heat with a canopy of green and contributed to the beauty of the city's parks and boulevards.

Then in 1958, the Dutch elm disease infected the city's special tree. The results were devastating. In 1963 alone, over 13,000 trees died.

In 1962, alarmed city officials brought Frank Vaydik, an expert on elm blight, to the city as a consultant. He recommended a program that he personally implemented later as park director. Vaydik's plan called for identifying diseased trees, spraying them or removing them, and replanting with a different species of tree. When DDT, the chemical used for spraying, was banned and no other insecticide worked, Kansas City's urban foresters controlled the disease by removing infected trees and eliminating breeding places for the elm bark beetle.

Before 1958, trees not on park land were supervised by the Public Works Department. But in an effort to professionalize horticultural efforts, the park board took over responsibility for all trees on the city's streets and park land. This administrative change was in place when the elm blight struck.

According to George Eib, now manager of horticultural services for Parks and Recreation, his responsibility covers about 540,000 trees: 40,000 on boulevards and parkways, 250,000 on other city streets, and an estimated 250,000 in developed and undeveloped park areas.

"Our urban foresters get to know these trees like individuals,"

Of all the American elms which graced Independence Boulevard (shown here in 1909), only two survived the Dutch elm disease which killed nearly 70,000 Kansas City trees following the onset of the blight in the late 1950s. To replace them, Christine Buisman elms first were planted but they turned out to be poor street trees. They are now being replaced by Rosehill ash trees.

Kansas City boasts more than 130 varieties of trees, beautiful in every season. Here ice glitters on trees along the banks of the Blue River.

Eib says. "They value them and want to protect them. When trees are taken out of context and put in an urban environment, they must compete for nutrients and light. Some trees do better in certain areas than do others."

Despite the city's affection for the American elm, Eib said foresters learned from the devastation caused by the elm bark beetle that many species of trees need to be planted so new diseases can't destroy the entire tree population.

"In our present reforestry program," he says, "we plant one mile of the same species—like the sweet gum or the Rose Hill ash—then we switch to another species." Each tree has its own character and growth pattern which determine where it will be planted.

Citizens helped combat the Dutch elm disease when they approved an earnings tax in 1963. Some of that money was used in an all-out effort to banish the blight. In 1966, Vaydik reported losses at 2.9 percent compared with 10.6 percent in 1963. In 1969, however, losses jumped again and the next year, the board received a bleak report blaming lack of funds for the inability of the forestry division to halt the spread of the disease. In 1971, the city council committed $500,000 to fight the disease and plant new trees. The goal was 5,000 new trees each year for the next ten years to cover losses and put trees in new areas of the city.

According to Eib, the goal is still 5,000 new trees a year. The park board remains committed to recapturing the look and feel of the forested city that Nelson, Meyer and Kessler envisioned and planned.

Neighborhoods provide much of the impetus for the natural look in the city. Michael Malyn, now manager of the planning services division, says when park designers seek advice about developing park property in neighborhoods, more and more residents are saying, 'Just leave it alone, leave it as natural as it can be. Take out the poison ivy, put up a sign and a picnic table and that will be plenty, thank you.'

"I attribute this attitude to increased value being placed on trees, the natural state of the land, the wildlife, and so on," Malyn says. "We are honoring those requests."

The war on the Dutch elm disease was hard fought and ultimately successful. In 1982, the city experienced the lowest percentage of trees lost since the battle began. Today, according to Eib, only one percent of the city's total tree population dies from any cause.

One of Kansas City's noble trees is located just south of the Swope Interpretative Center in Swope Park. Called the Swope Park Crittenden Oak, the tree has a trunk four feet in diameter and was once tall and stately.

This tree grew from an acorn with a prestigious "family tree." According to W. I. Ayres, former draftsman for the parks, the Swope Park Crittenden oak is the great-grandson of the Charter Oak, a huge tree that once stood in Hartford, Connecticut. Tradition claims that in 1687 a state legislator hid the state's original charter in the oak tree to keep the English governor from seizing it.

King James II of England sent Sir Edmund Andros to Hartford to capture the Connecticut charter and take control of the colony. During a lengthy legislative debate one night, the candles suddenly went out and Joseph Wadsworth of Hartford took advantage of the darkness to grab the charter and hide it in the tree. Safe from capture, the charter remained the state's supreme law until Connecticut adopted a new constitution in 1818.

In 1909, Sen. John Jordan Crittenden of Kentucky lived in a home with an avenue of oak trees, all "sons" of the Charter Oak. He sent an acorn from one of them to the National Botanical Garden which grew the Crittenden Peace Oak, grandson of the Charter Oak. When his nephew, Thomas T. Crittenden, former governor of Missouri, asked for acorns from that tree, Senator Crittenden sent two, which the governor planted in Swope Park in 1908.

Only one of the Charter Oak great-grandsons lived. A beautiful shade tree, the oak was admired and cherished until 1985 when lightening struck and badly disfigured the once majestic oak. According to George Eib, the tree cannot live much longer. "But we have many acorns from it that we will plant in Swope Park," he says, assuring the continuation of an arboreal family line that dates from the 1600s.

During dry summer months the concrete bed of Brush Creek made a natural theater for concerts that attracted thousands of people. Development plans for the creek call for an amphitheater down stream from the Country Club Plaza.

CHAPTER VIII

Parks as Playgrounds

When the weather is fine, Kansas City parks and playgrounds are abuzz with people of all ages enjoying both organized and spontaneous recreation. In fact, it is hard to imagine a time when parklands were not used by active people. But there was such a time.

During the nineteenth century, land planners such as Olmsted, Meyer and Kessler believed urban parks should be for quiet renewal and refreshment; not rambunctious play. As far as children were concerned, planners theorized that appealing surroundings alone would properly educate and socialize them.

For many years, Kessler scoffed at "so-called playgrounds having a lot of expensive directors and sociological workers." But he was bucking a powerful new movement in reform-minded America, and eventually even he became convinced of the need for playgrounds and more play activities in the parks.

As early as 1901, Kansas City women's clubs advocated "vacation playgrounds," to conserve the health and morals of the children. In a letter to the park board, Mrs. John C. Gage, mother of John B. Gage, reform mayor, wrote that the clubwomen felt "youth has equal rights with age in the use of our pleasure grounds." The newspaper chimed in. "The hot weather of the last week has emphasized a great need in Kansas City, the need of the public playgrounds for the small children — small pleasure grounds at accessible distances — little oases for youthful recreation in a desert of brick and asphalt," wrote the *Kansas City Star* in July 1907.

Gradually the park board accepted the new thinking, and in 1909 hired playground directors and chose playground sites for the summer season. Two years later, D.J. Haff, as president of the board, called for playgrounds within walking distance of every resident and said, "We have kept constantly in mind the thought that not for this day and generation only are we planning, but for all succeeding generations."

During the early years of this century, the emerging playground movement often was at odds with the planners influenced by the City Beautiful movement. Funds for beautification could be derailed if playground advocates wanted space and equipment. The two movements soon discovered, however, they could jointly establish a sense of community, effect social action and blend beauty with efficiency and utility.

In Kansas City, controlling the children was a high priority for Elenore Canny, the first director at Holmes Square playground. "Rules prohibiting children with dirty faces or uncombed hair to participate in any of the games were made and enforced. This had the desired effect," she reported to the park board at the end of her first season.

She had more trouble controlling outsiders, she said, and solved the problem by joining the police department so, according to a *Kansas City Journal* editorial, "if any unmannerly tough disturbed the enjoyment of the children, she could arrest him and let him meditate upon social ethics at the Workhouse for a few weeks, until he learns to respect the rights of others."

Although undertaken tentatively, the first organized summer play programs were so successful that, the board voted on February 20, 1911 to create a Recreation Commission composed of one member each from the park board, public welfare, the Board of Education, the Playground Association of America, and both houses of the Common Council.

Eventually the Recreation Division of the Welfare Department administered the programs. According to Mary Edith Lillis, who began working full-time with the department in 1953, "We were really working with the poor, the needy — the forgotten groups. So that meant working without anything, without any supplies, under conditions we all accepted as necessary to get our job done. It was a giveaway program because people couldn't afford to pay. Over time, we did find there were things people would pay for.

"After World War II," she recalls, "a lot of things began to be formalized. Some [things] stayed under different umbrellas for awhile because the park department had the land, the pools and things

Surefire summertime fun in Kansas City means fishing at Troost Lake at The Paseo and Twenty-eighth Street.

Lakes and lagoons in parks throughout the city attract both people and ducks. Here a fisherman and friend try their luck at Lake of the Woods in Swope Park.

The natural beauty of Swope Park surrounds golfers playing the two public courses contained within the park.

of that nature, while we at the Welfare Department did the playground and community centers in the poorer sections of the city."

In the early 1960s, governmental leaders began to articulate concern about the physical fitness of Americans, especially youth. School programs began to examine their physical education programs and communities began to look toward city-wide initiatives to improve opportunities for physical activity. Nationwide there was a movement to consolidate major organizations concerned with parks and with recreation. In this climate, a merger of the recreation division and the park board seemed desirable.

On October 10, 1962, the board passed a resolution asking that the welfare division's public recreation program be placed under the park department. The merger required a vote by the citizens to change the city charter. At a city election in November 1966, voters approved the charter change and the board passed a resolution, amending its name to the Board of Parks & Recreation.

The board lost no time in announcing an expanded program that included nineteen new playgrounds; eleven more baseball diamonds; and new swimming, tennis, biking and archery facilities. Since then, recreational programming has grown to embrace more sports and games, arts and crafts, dance, music, drama, puppetry and special events for senior citizens and people with disabilities.

The outdoor education programs developed during the early 1960s and expanded later to include archaeology programs at Line Creek and the Shoal Creek historic programs have been nationally recognized by the Department of Interior, according to Patti Kortkamp, supervisor of Outdoor Education and Historic Sites. "Over the past thirty years," she says, "one million citizens have experienced the impact in the Kansas City environs of wildlife, prehistoric cultures and early American history."

In recent years, the board also has greatly expanded recreational opportunities for Kansas Citians by co-planning events with major cultural institutions of the city, such as the Kansas City Symphony, the Kansas City Jazz Commission, the State Ballet of Missouri, Bruce R. Watkins Cultural Arts Center and organizations representing the city's many ethnic heritages. The board also sponsors appearances by nationally known lecturers, as well as musicians and other artists.

After Kansas City's civil disorders of 1968, Frank Vaydik suggested schools should be used for after-school recreational programs sponsored by parks and recreation. Working in cooperation with Kansas City's Board of Education, the park board designed an Open Door Program to use school buildings for educational and recre-

ational purposes. Starting with a few schools, the program grew. By February 1974, it claimed participation by fifty schools, five school districts and 300,000 participants. Dr. Robert Hodge, then president of the board, encouraged the program because, "the facilities are all owned by the same taxpayers."

∾

Parks for Everyone

Looking back, it seems appropriate that some of the most significant battle lines in the campaign for racial equality in Kansas City were drawn in parks and on playgrounds. By definition and design, the parks were meant for all people to enjoy, yet custom and regulation prohibited black citizens from full use of the parks. The issue was especially heated over playgrounds and pools. Black parents wanted parks for everyone, but they especially wanted recreational opportunities available to their children.

Across the country, racial barriers of all kinds began to be challenged after World War II. The triumph against oppression overseas was followed by a struggle for racial integration here at home. Black Americans believed they had been patient long enough, and the time had come for total integration into the life of the community.

The Missouri constitution mandated separation of the races, and Kansas Citians had never known integrated schools, public facilities or recreational programs in the parks. Now new values arose, and the majority community was alarmed and wary in the face of sudden and drastic changes.

In the late 1940s and early 1950s, the local chapter of the National Association for the Advancement of Colored People (NAACP) complained often to the park board about park facilities being denied them. "For a long time," recalled Lucile Bluford, editor of the *Kansas City Call*, "black citizens were welcome at Swope Park only on Watermelon Hill right across from the zoo. If a black family tried to picnic in other parts of the park, rangers and police would come by and tell them to move. We had a lot of articles in the *Call* about that harassment."

In responding to the *Call*, John Moore, board president from 1940 to 1948, described the board's policy of race separation as an "unwritten law" upheld by "custom and tradition," and said it would be maintained in all park property.

Blacks living near parks in largely white neighborhoods were

More than 40 shelter houses in 27 different parks are maintained for the enjoyment of Kansas Citians. When this one was photographed in the 1950s, the shelter houses were regular spots for summer parties in the days before many homes had air-conditioning.

Hidden Valley Park provides one of hundreds of fine picnic spots in the parks system.

More than 100 public tennis courts — about 20 percent of them lighted — dot the parks. Many, like this one on the Country Club Plaza, also have practice boards.

sometimes given permission to enjoy all facilities except the swimming pool. But they wanted to swim, too, especially in the beautiful pool at Swope Park.

In June 1951, the NAACP threatened to take the park board to court if it did not open Swope Park pool to blacks. The board repeated its policy of providing "equal and adequate swimming pool and other park facilities for all citizens of Kansas City" and said the policy would continue without change.

Early in 1952, the NAACP filed suit, and the board responded by closing the Swope Park pool for the summer season. By the next spring, the lower courts decided in favor of integration, but the City Council appealed the decision to the U.S. Supreme Court. They did, however, recommend the pool be opened for the 1953 season while litigation was pending. But the board refused to change its policy until the Supreme Court rendered a decision.

On March 31, 1954, after the Supreme Court refused to review the decision of the U.S. Court of Appeals of the Eighth District in favor of the NAACP, the board adopted a resolution opening the pool to everyone. The NAACP then asked for integration of the Grove swimming pool and the Garrison wading pool, but the board refused, saying the court action affected only the Swope park pool. The next year, however, after appeals from the Commission on Human Relations, the board integrated all pools.

Golf Course #1, now Swope Memorial Golf Course, at Swope Park was the last bastion of segregation in the park system. According to Ilus Davis, mayor from 1963 to 1971, some golfers were using part of the locker room as a private club. "They were fairly outspoken," Davis said, and resistant to integration, but within a year after Davis took office, the course opened to all golfers.

When the black community exploded in riots in the summer of 1968, destroying property in their own neighborhoods, Kansas City was stunned and puzzled. As Robert Kipp, former city manager, explains, the white majority couldn't understand what was happening because they believed they tried to give blacks a fair deal and wanted to do even more. "During that period [there] was a sort of boiling over of feelings, deep and justified feelings, [from blacks]

that 'we no longer want to be treated that way.' The majority community couldn't understand that being full-fledged partners, participants in the process, was what the minority community wanted. Membership on the park board would have been an example."

City officials in Kansas City were caught off-guard because they did not grasp the radical character of the changes needed. But the mayor did. According to Kipp, Davis was out in front on these issues in Kansas City: "Ilus Davis was more clearly the person who said to the community in many ways, 'This is something we can't live with,' and he spent his political capital on these issues," Kipp says. "He advocated the 'Open Accommodations' ordinance back when it was extremely unpopular. Many of his associates couldn't understand why he would take such a radical position, but he was very forthright and very direct. He exercised real leadership in the matter of racial progress. He did what he thought was right, and it was right."

In 1971, Mayor Charles Wheeler recognized the importance of black representation on the park board and appointed Harold L. Holliday, Jr. A year later, when Jeremiah Cameron, another black Kansas Citian, replaced Holliday, the minority community had a clear and commanding voice on the park board.

The appreciation of the black community for the city's parks and boulevards continued in the years that followed and support intensified and became more focused. After the dedication of the Spirit of Freedom Fountain, the community concentrated on memorializing two of its most beloved: baseball hero Satchel Paige and Bernard Powell, a local political leader.

In 1982, the old Catholic Youth Organization stadium at Fifty-first Street and Swope Parkway was dedicated to Paige and with significant contributions from the black community was completely renovated. A memorial fountain in Spring Valley Park was dedicated to Powell in August 1988.

The black community, especially the clergy, worked diligently to build a memorial at Truman Road and The Paseo to Rev. John Williams, a black police chaplain. It was dedicated in August 1991.

The Muse of the Missouri, a beautiful bronze goddess representing the spirit of the Missouri River, glistens in the sunlight as she casts a net over the Main Street island between Eighth and Ninth Streets. Always an emblem of this city's important connection to the Missouri River, today the Muse suggests a reawakened interest in the river front and river market areas. Created by New York sculptor Wheeler Williams, the Muse fountain was given to the city by James Kemper, Sr. in honor of his son, Lt. David W. Kemper, killed in action in World War II.

CHAPTER IX

A Heritage Revisited

Wide rivers and fertile land were important to this region's early development. In the 1970s, the park board recognized the importance of the area's river heritage with an ambitious project and at the same time claimed for posterity a piece of property that recalled the wild, rich land which first drew farmers to settle this region. After Kansas City became a railroad center in the late 1860s, most citizens turned their backs on the river that had been a source of mobility and livelihood. Although its commercial life continued in barge traffic, occasional cruising river boats and a few fishermen, the river was largely ignored.

During the years when Dr. Robert Hodge was president of the park board, recalls former board secretary R.E. Soper, "We had a project called River Reach designed by John See, staff architect, a plan for improvement to the river front, but that never got off the ground. Everyone wants to do something about the river front, but nobody gets around to it."

In 1965, however, at Frank Vaydik's urging, the park board voted to develop a riverfront park. Early in 1967, the board entered into an agreement with the federal government to develop eighty acres of riverfront property west of the Chouteau Bridge. The area was historically significant as part of the Lewis and Clark Trail and, later, as the site of early French settlement of this area by members of the Chouteau family and their employees to develop trade routes for the St. Louis-based family fur business.

In September 1970, the board dedicated the park at a celebration complete with boat races on the river. The next year, the park board asked the City Council for authority to extend the boundaries of the park to include 540 acres east of the bridge. Ultimately, Riverfront Park encompassed 955 acres.

By 1976, the park had a boat ramp and was the site of the city's official celebration of the nation's bicentennial. "Hundreds of thousands of people came down," said Richard Marr, then president of the park board. "Riverfront Park was a great place because of the openness. My kids and I went and participated in bubble gum blowing contests and log rolling. It was just good old-fashioned fun."

The area was ideal, too, for devoted birdwatchers. An estimated forty to fifty varieties of birds live in the cottonwood trees and grasslands along the river banks. The area is so rich in all kinds of native wildlife that, in 1982, the Missouri Conservation Commission asked permission to use part of it as a wildlife resource area for twenty years.

But in 1983, the city's Department of Health reported to the park board that Environmental Protection Agency (EPA) studies revealed possible hazardous waste in the parkland. Two years later, the board temporarily closed the park following a report of traces of lead in the soil. To meet EPA clean-up standards, the board needed $500,000 to make the site usable, but it only had $300,000.

Riverfront Park remains closed, but current park director Terry Dopson says about 200 acres of the park should be ready for use by 1993. A three-foot cap on top of the ground would meet Health Department standards for reusing the area for recreational purposes, according to Dopson.

The park board has been part of a planning initiative to revitalize the area around the city market at Fifth and Delaware for mixed use development. Now well into its first phase, the River Market development is attracting new businesses and residents to a charming area of brick sidewalks, renovated buildings, and loft living in adapted warehouse spaces. This interest bodes well for the future of the riverfront, one of the city's most potentially exciting public-use areas.

About the same time that the Riverfront Park was under development, the board was presented an exceptional opportunity to have as a park a wooded and gullied piece of property that strongly resembles this region as it was when the first major immigration of settlers arrived in the early 1850s. Businessman and philanthropist Jerry Smith offered the city the chance to purchase his farm at 135th Street and Prospect Avenue for use as a future park.

The Smith farm features a three-acre lake and wooded draws

SHOAL CREEK VILLAGE

During the past seventeen years, Parks staff and committed volunteers have turned special skills and interests to recreating a nineteenth century Missouri village at Hodge Park. They work alongside persons interested in historic preservation who spend hours locating and researching old buildings that can be moved. Shoal Creek Village represents a cross-section of social, commercial, and economic life as it was lived in Missouri between 1821 and 1880.

The village evolves from a master plan created by Michael Malyn, now manager of planning services, after a Clay County resident, Reed Byers, offered park director Frank Vaydik an old log cabin. "Vaydik contacted me and said 'What would you do if you had a log cabin'?" says Malyn. At the time, Malyn was working on Hodge Park and he told Vera Eldridge, Clay County historian, of the log cabin find. "She knew of this building and told me of others threatened by developers, so I submitted a proposal to Vaydik to do an entire village of thirty buildings."

To date, according to Malyn, park employees and volunteers have restored fifteen buildings including the log cabin, a mill, church, blacksmith shop, school, mule barn, general store, mansion and jail. "We found the calaboose in Missouri City. Their city council tried to restore it but in the process, the building collapsed, so they were happy to have us take it. Fortunately, we had earlier photographed it and measured it."

The process of moving an old building involves researching it, photographing and measuring it, then taking it apart and putting it back together. In the case of the beautiful brick mansion which once belonged to a family named Thornton, park employees had to move it one brick at a time. "We had to redo the engineering so it could be used as a public building. We also had to conceal all modern conveniences such as bathrooms, air conditioning, heating and electrical outlets so they wouldn't detract from its historic value," Malyn says.

In recent years, volunteers from the Northland Assistance League have designed furnishings, searched for antiques, and planned the annual June festival when a living history presentation shows visitors how Missourians lived in the nineteenth century. A special group, Friends of Shoal Creek Village, formed out of this league includes tireless volunteers Susan Perry, Faye Werner, Jan Kauk, Irene Thomas, Judy Chastain and others who concentrate on continuing the preservation of this heritage.

Living history demonstrations at Shoal Creek Village include periodic Civil War re-enactments.

that are home to deer, rabbits, raccoons, birds and other wildlife. According to Frank Vaydik, the property might be the last large piece of land to be acquired in one piece. "It's beautiful land," he says, "and ideal for a park to serve an area of the city that is rapidly building up."

In 1975, Kansas City's City Council voted overwhelmingly to purchase the 360-acre farm east of the Blue River and south of 135th Street, at a bargain price. Smith contributed one-quarter of the purchase price and a federal grant underwrote half, making the city's cost for the remaining ninety acres a nominal sum by usual standards.

The federal funds came from the Land and Water Conservation Fund created during the 1960s to allocate money from the leasing of off-shore oil drilling rights for the purchase and development of park land. In this way, as one natural resource was depleted, the government could enhance another.

The Jerry Smith farm is atop developed oil fields that run underneath much of the Kansas City region. In earlier years, hundreds of oil wells operated in the area that includes the Smith farm. Many had not been active for years. In 1983, however, when the price of oil skyrocketed, a lot of speculators created oil field explorations as a tax dodge. Speculators approached the park board for permission to drill, but Jerry Darter, Parks and Recreation director at the time, was reluctant to disturb the area's natural beauty. Hoping for a negative response, he asked for the state of Missouri's required permission — which fortunately was refused. The positive quality of the farmland was retained.

Master plans for the park include a working farm, a unique woodcock breeding area, picnic areas and other park facilities. Like Swope Park, the full potential of Jerry Smith farm as a park will be realized by Kansas Citians of the future who will find in its rural treat a glimpse of some of the best of the past.

Parks attract visitors in all weather. Here hardy mountain bicyclists enjoy the winter scenery in Minor Park.

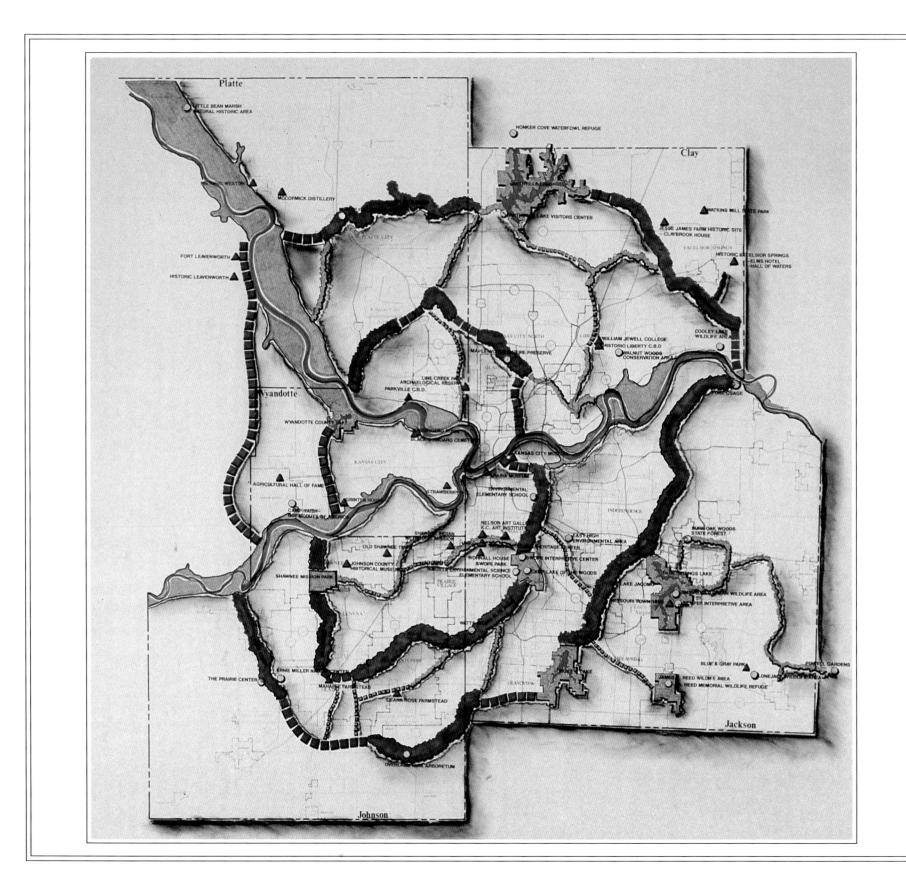

GREENWAY LEGEND

 MAJOR RIVERS   VALLEY FLOODPLAIN AND FLOODWAY ASSOCIATED WITH THE MISSOURI AND KANSAS RIVERS

 STREAM CORRIDORS   COMPRISED OF NATURAL LINEAR SYSTEMS OF WOODLANDS AND WATER COURSES INCLUDING EXISTING GREENWAYS

 UPLAND CONNECTIONS   LINKAGES COMPRISED OF BOULEVARDS. ABANDONED RAIL RIGHTS OF WAY AND HIGH POINTS BETWEEN WATER COURSES

 CULTURAL DISCOVERY CENTER   EDUCATIONAL OPPORTUNITY FOR UNDERSTANDING CULTURAL DIVERSITY

 NATURAL DISCOVERY CENTER   EDUCATIONAL OPPORTUNITY FOR UNDERSTANDING NATURAL DIVERSITY

 **Concept** for the
Kansas City Metropolitan Greenway System

A Community Assistance Team Project
American Society of Landscape Architects, Prairie Gateway Chapter

Concept for the Kansas City Metropolitan Greenway System, 1991

Over the past thirty years, people of all ages have taken part in historical and environmental programs in the parks, planned to allow the past to teach valuable lessons for the future. Shoal Creek Village, a reconstructed nineteenth century rural village in Hodge Park, is a good example of these programs.

CHAPTER X

New Directions

In May 1979, newly elected mayor Richard Berkley introduced his choices for the park board: Anita Gorman, the first woman board member; LeeVertis Swinton, a lawyer; and Kansas City's former city manager, L.P. Cookingham, who served as board president. Of these three, only Gorman served during Berkley's entire twelve-year administration. Through that long period, she exhibited strong leadership skills, working effectively with five different commissioners on complex issues challenging the board. At a critical juncture, she helped turn the attention of the other commissioners in a new direction.

For ninety years, the park board had struggled with funding, depending on an unpredictable mix of city allocations, private gifts and government grants. In many ways, the financial history of the parks is a study in public/private partnerships and exemplifies the ability of Kansas Citians to get things done even when the team required is an unexpected yoking. But in 1983, the parks faced a dire threat.

That year, the Missouri Supreme Court interpreted the Hancock Amendment, aimed at holding the lid on state spending, to mean that the park board could not raise user fees to maintain park facilities. The board knew the parks were in jeopardy. As Mrs. Gorman explains, "We had been told that we were exempt from that, so we had continued to raise our user fees as we always had." The Supreme Court of the state of Missouri rolled back the regulation and demanded refund of the fees to the public, but, of course, the parks board had already used the money.

Robert Kipp, city manager, and Joanne Collins, chairman of the council's finance committee and a city councilman, told the park board it was in financial trouble and asked what the commissioners intended to do. The failing health of Mrs. Perry Cookingham kept the board president busy and cast Anita Gorman into the spokesperson's role. Gorman told the council, "We're going to have an election, and the people will vote for this."

City officials warned that with the country in the recession of the early 1980s, an election to raise taxes could fail. But the board said, "We have to try." Kipp says, "Fortunately, we have always had some individuals with greater vision and with foresight, and most recently it's really been Anita Gorman and the other commissioners saying, 'we're going to take our case to the people because there's a case to be made.'"

As a non-partisan governmental entity, the park board had never asked people directly for funds. "It was a brand-new thing," says Gorman, "but I told them 'this has got to be a campaign. We've got to go to people and ask for their support to let us continue to do what we'd always done.'"

Signs went up all over town. "Our people were inexperienced campaigners," says Gorman, "but the signs were so good the elected politicians asked us if they could have them when it was over.

"We won that election by about fifty-four percent. That was a turning point. Now it seems insignificant, but at that time it was the difference between balancing our budget and really being in a terrible situation. It also gave us the opportunity to go directly to the people, and that helped us later when we began to form other partnerships."

The voters responded again in 1986 to the leadership of Gorman, who became president that year after the retirement of Cookingham. By an overwhelming majority, Kansas Citians voted to increase the park maintenance levy from ten cents on a hundred dollars assessed evaluation to fifty cents and the boulevard front foot tax (which had not been raised since 1925) from ten cents a front foot to one dollar. With the increased funds, the park board was again able to hire enough labor to mow, pick up trash, sweep the parkways and boulevards, prune and plant trees, treat weeds and plant flower beds.

The board's new directions were having visible effects. When Kansas Citians saw their parks and boulevards taking on a fresh look, they experienced a rebirth of interest. During the 1980s, a $5 billion construction boom raised new commercial buildings throughout

Park employees post pertinent reminders of what lies beneath snow covered park lawns and what Kansas Citians can look forward to after winter has retreated.

Apartment dwellers and others who work and live on the Country Club Plaza appreciate the jogging trail in Mill Creek along J.C. Nichols Parkway. The park was improved with private contributions and in a fine example of public/private partnership for a better parks system.

Every year thousands of tulips planted by the parks staff create a breathtaking display along boulevards and in parks.

the metroplex. Residents were elated at the city's progress but in the face of so much commercial growth, the treasure of trees and open space began to seem all the more precious.

∾

More Partnerships

Voters' positive responses to the park's needs set the park board to thinking about other ways citizens could help with the upkeep of the parks and boulevards. Was it possible, they asked themselves, that people might care enough to arm themselves with paint brushes and litter bags and give their time to help with park maintenance? In the fall of 1974, a group of citizens had swarmed over the grounds of the Nelson Art Gallery, sprucing them up before the arrival of the prestigious Chinese Archaeological Exhibition. Could this kind of event be encouraged?

Over the years, willing volunteers have been important to a number of park projects. One of the most significant single contributions was made by Lillie F. Kelsay, who researched and wrote a history of Kansas City's historic and dedicatory monuments as a special gift to the board.

"Then one year," Michael Malyn recalls, "we had a lot of volunteers who had helped us and we wanted to get them into the flower show so we made badges that said 'V.I.P.' which stood for "Volunteers in Parks."'" The 'VIPs' were delighted. The next year, 1982, the park board formalized these efforts by establishing a "Volunteers in Parks" program.

James O'Shea, landscape architect for planning services, was instrumental in organizing hundreds of people who wanted to volunteer their services. Their efforts released trained park crews for heavier work. The park board provided the volunteer workers with tokens of appreciation: golf passes, free horseback rides or visits to the zoo, but the real reward, volunteers said, was in seeing that individuals could make a positive difference to the ongoing life of the parks.

In a parallel effort, Steve Lampone, manager of park services, worked with businesses and corporations who wanted to become involved in the program. Immediately after the program was formalized, dozens of volunteers from five corporations headquartered downtown (Crown Center Redevelopment, IBM, Mutual Benefit Life, Pershing Square and the Westin Crown Center Hotel) turned out to give neighboring Washington Square a thorough scrubbing.

Other private initiatives stimulated people to champion their parks and boulevards. The first such effort was the revitalization of Ward Parkway from Fifty-fifth to Fifth-ninth Streets. Concerned neighbors created an endowment fund within The Greater Kansas City Community Foundation to finance work along the parkway. Before long, other groups farther south on Ward Parkway were doing similar things.

At about the same time, Miller Nichols and Dr. Ben McAllister initiated the Mill Creek Park Association and established an endowment fund to enhance and maintain the park at Forty-seventh Street and J.C. Nichols Parkway. In the park, the association developed an exercise trail that is heavily used. To pay for it, "We raised $600,000 through gifts," says Nichols. "We kept about $100,000 and put it in the Kansas City Community Foundation to grow. That's now doubled, and we get contributions every year. Our agreement with the park board is that we contribute ninety percent of our earned income from the fund and invest it in the park each year. The park board likes it and the park's a credit to the city. This shows community involvement."

Another example of community involvement was the renovation of the Catholic Youth Organization stadium at Fifty-first Street and Swope Parkway. In 1982, the board dedicated the stadium to Kansas Citian Satchel Paige, the black baseball player who had been a sports legend since the 1940s.

"We dedicated it on a Saturday," recalls Ollie Gates, who replaced parks commissioner, Bruce Watkins, on the board after Watkins' death in 1980. "Satchel Paige was there with his oxygen and his wheelchair. He died that next Tuesday." At the dedication, Paige said, "This is the happiest day of my life."

The board considered renovating the stadium a priority because of the need for such a facility in that location and because the old stadium was an eyesore. "The neighbors joined in," Gates says, "because they were getting something ugly and raggedy out of the neighborhood." Led by the black community, many citizens helped with the campaign to raise funds for the stadium's rehabilitation. According to Lucile Bluford, editor of the *Kansas City Call,* "We thought of the idea of raising money a dollar at a time. We put it in the paper every week about mailing in a dollar or more, and we raised quite a little bit of money. Every week or two, I'd take the money down to the park board and give it to them. That was my first real relationship with the park board."

In addition to individuals, major Kansas City businesses and

Attention to detail in the maintenance of Kansas City parks and boulevards is a key reason for the fine reputation of the vast system.

The park board maintains park property at Forty-third Street and Broadway where Vietnam Veterans and friends have built a moving memorial and fountains, dedicated in 1983.

Usually a trickle in its concrete bed, Brush Creek at flood stage threatens the property of merchants and residents along its banks. A flood control plan known as the Brush Creek Beautification Project will link the Country Club Plaza area with eastern Kansas City. A walkway and a series of small bodies of water from State Line Road to the Blue River will enhance the cultural and recreational life in Kansas City.

corporations contributed. The stadium project was completed in the fall of 1983, and in December 1984, at their annual dinner, the park commissioners presented a special award to Lucile Bluford for her leadership in the stadium fund drive.

Over time, more and more people embraced the idea of sharing the responsibility for park renovation or upkeep. One of the largest neighborhood efforts at rehabilitation involved Cliff Drive, which threads its way through the splendid greenery along the curving road overlooking the Missouri River in Kessler Park. Designed by George Kessler before the turn of the century, the drive was a diamond in a rough and natural setting. For years it reflected the best of the city's beautiful park system: handsome stone out-croppings, abundant trees of many varieties, stretches of sheltered drive punctuated by overlooks with beautiful views. But as age crumbled walls and curbings, people began using the park as a dumping ground.

In April 1986, with the aid of Councilman Frank Palermo, the board set aside $445,000 to renovate Cliff Drive. A month later, hundreds of volunteers from six northeast neighborhood associations, spearheaded by Carl DiCapo, a park commissioner who was a northeast area native, dug out and carted away debris. To assure that the drive would not revert to a dumping ground, residents created an effective neighborhood watch group.

Also in 1986, the board established another important alliance with citizens, the on-going "Adopt a Park" program. Arbor Villa Park at Sixty-sixth Terrace and Main Street was the beginning. The local neighborhood organization asked to take greater responsibility in maintaining their park and the park board agreed to allot them funds that would have been spent anyway. The group added funds to privately contract work on the park. Now both the neighborhood and the park board are delighted with the results.

According to commissioner Ollie Gates, "People are starting to look at our city in a small-town sense, saying 'this is my town, and how can I help,' rather than saying 'well, this is Kansas City, and I'll just take from it.'"

❧

From Open Sewer to Cultural Confluent

Early inhabitants of this region, from nomadic tribes of Native Americans to nineteenth century settlers brought west by the promise of land and gold, were enticed to stay partly by the number of clear running streams that crisscrossed the region. The streams provided water for farming and milling, and eventually for carrying away the effluents of city life.

Brush Creek, which cuts across eastern Kansas, enters Kansas City just west of the Country Club Plaza, then threads its way east to the Blue River, had lost its sparkling value and become a problem demanding a creative solution.

No longer the pretty stream along which Daniel Boone's son trapped beaver, by the 1930s it had become a public nuisance, carrying waste and raw sewage to the river. The solution offered by Boss Tom Pendergast and his Ready-Mixed Concrete Company was to force the sewer into a narrow bed flanked by reinforced cement. It set off a loud protest from outraged citizens, but he built it anyway.

In time, Kansas Citians learned to tolerate this strange looking creek and even to take advantage of its concrete bed. Because the creek was usually dry, public concerts could be held in the creek with the banks creating a natural amphitheater setting. But the creek wasn't always dry. Heavy rains could raise it to the top of its banks. As more asphalt and concrete covered land along the creek's southern basin, run-off increased because rain couldn't be absorbed into the ground. In September 1977, too much concrete both in Johnson County and on the creek bed proved fatal. Moisture from days of heavy rains had nowhere to go but up. The creek flooded, causing the loss of twenty-two lives and tens of millions of dollars in property damage particularly in the Country Club Plaza area. Storm water drainage in general and Brush Creek in particular became hot topics.

"The '77 flood lit a fire under us all," says City Manager Dave Olson. Nonetheless, despite the damage, the people of Kansas City defeated a bond issue for flood control in an election held immediately after the flood.

Through its Corps of Engineers, the federal government offered to pay seventy-five percent of a flood control program. Kansas City was able to guarantee fifty million dollars by using future income from a sales tax in a plan proposed by then-Councilman Emanuel Cleaver II.

"The Cleaver plan came out of a frustration, an inability to come up with a local share, as well as a real opportunity to turn Brush Creek into more than a flood control project and make it a very nice walkway," says Olson. The Corps of Engineers' plan, however, called for a deep, wide channel with no beautification and little or no pedestrian access.

"Parks and Recreation got into the act," says Michael Malyn,

THE DESIGNED ENVIRONMENT

No one could dispute that this region was endowed with fortunate gifts of nature. But the combination of rocks, water, trees and meadows has been transformed beyond simple (and barely habitable) wilderness by the vision and dedication of planners, architects and landscape architects. In a continuing tradition, designers have not only made Kansas City's parks, boulevards, fountains, and public places, they have also made them beautiful.

The visions of designers have been the means by which the public has known what 18th century poet (and lover of parks) Alexander Pope called "nature to advantage dressed." Like a door to the secret garden, designed spaces and built forms can lead us into the experience of nature and enrich the experience of urban life.

From the earliest plans of George Kessler to the metropolitan greenway system created in 1991 by representatives of more than 85 municipal and parks jurisdictions working with the Prairie Gateway Chapter of the American Society of Landscape Architects, designers have seen the special opportunities in Kansas City's natural attributes.

Throughout Kansas City, the work of designers and planners is everywhere, often so integral to our perception of the city that it seems hardly designed at all, but rather always to have been

there. Parks, squares, courtyards, boulevards, fountains, bridges, walls, buildings — even the very best are too numerous to list, as are the names of their designers. But some names have assumed nearly legendary status: Kessler, of course; Henry Van Brunt (the August Meyer residence); Walter Root and George Siemens (the Penn Valley Park Maintenance Building); Louis Curtiss (the Folly Theater); Thomas Wight (the Swope Memorial); Edward Buehler Delk (Starlight Theater); Edward Tanner (much of the Country Club Plaza, working with Delk); and Sid and Herbert Hare, the father and son team responsible for so many of the city's public places, such as Loose Park.

Many contemporary architecture, engineering and landscape firms — both local and national in reputation — have worked on developing modern Kansas City's public spaces and parks. Their efforts reveal the ongoing truth in a remark made by the nineteenth century landscape master, Frederick L. Olmsted, "It is a common error to regard a park as something . . . complete in itself." Today the work of a hundred years of good design blends the park experience with the city experience in ways that are unmistakably Kansas City, and unmistakably fine.

In 1987, the architectural team of Daniel Urban Kiley and Jaquelin Taylor Robertson began to design the Henry Moore Sculpture Garden, dedicated in 1989. Kiley has said, "This garden shall stand as a testament of our time and our presence within the cosmos. This place shall be independently strong and powerful in its overall impact. ..."

current manager of planning services, "because it's our property for the most part down through the Brush Creek channel, and we felt there was a real opportunity to develop a flood control plan that could be gorgeous."

"I want to say that the Brush Creek project is strictly a park department initiative. They had the idea, went down to San Antonio, talked to the people and came back with some realistic planning and then got others of us interested in it," says then-Mayor Richard Berkley.

"Typically, if engineers are solving flood control, that's all they solve," says Jerry Darter, who was park director at the time the Brush Creek project began to be developed. "They may care about aesthetics, but if it's not part of their project, it can be left behind.

"We talked to Al Groves, who had significant involvement in the San Antonio River project, and asked him to come up and take a preliminary look. He gave us plenty of ideas. The Corps said the ideas couldn't be done, but eventually the city commissioned a huge model, built in Vicksburg, Mississippi, and Miller Nichols hauled a whole bunch of them down there to see that."

The Corps had no accurate mathematical way to check design assumptions, and park officials felt that a scale model would enable them to come up with the best plan. The model of Brush Creek was 440 feet long, big enough to walk through.

The turning point came in 1988 when the Corps agreed that the park proposal, which included dams to control flooding and provide recreational water bodies, could be beautiful as well as beneficial.

"If the federal government stays on its schedule, we're looking at 1995 to accomplish the flood control aspects of the plan," says Malyn. "Parks and Recreation and the city of Kansas City must follow right behind engineering contracts with beautification contracts."

"There are a lot of cultural resources [along the creek], from the Bruce R. Watkins Cultural Heritage Center at one end to the Nelson-Atkins Museum at the other, with the Plaza, Ward Parkway, UMKC, Midwest Research Institution. We see then another layer of cultural development that we're calling the 'cultural corridor project' where we can encourage different kinds of arts activities, performing arts, outdoor displays, all in a programmed format," says Malyn.

The Corps will start south of the art gallery, with excavations that will bring Brush Creek to the surface. Parks and recreation will begin beautifying there. According to the designs, the William Volker Memorial Fountain will be moved to the south side of Brush Creek where it will be seen along Volker Boulevard.

The redesigned Theis Park and a highlighted Volker Fountain will relate aesthetically to the Henry A. Moore Sculpture Garden, which opened June 4, 1989, on seventeen acres on the south grounds of the Nelson-Atkins Museum of Art. The Moore Collection, on extended loan to the museum by Mr. and Mrs. Donald J. Hall, comprises nearly sixty works by Moore, the largest collection outside his native England. The garden was a project of the museum, the Hall Family Foundations, and the park board, and it features twelve sculptures by Henry Moore, considered one of the great sculptors of the twentieth century. His large, non-representational forms blend perfectly into a setting of gradual terraces and looping paths with beautiful flowers, trees and vining ground cover on the museum grounds.

Hall explains that the Henry Moore collection came to the attention of the Hall Family Foundations when George Ablah, a Wichita businessman, who had sold a number of his Moore pieces to Japanese collectors, made the body of his collection, the largest outside England, available. "We thought it was an opportunity to do something special and unique in Kansas City for visitors and citizens alike," said Hall. "We went ahead and bought it and went about the task of locating it at the gallery."

The Moore sculpture garden is a cultural enhancement that adds to the promise of the Brush Creek project. The project is also sparking urban redevelopment ideas in the Town Fork area between the proposed Bruce R. Watkins Roadway and Elmwood, an area previously undeveloped because of the danger of flooding. The Brush Creek project is expected to make a vital economic center of activity in the 1990s.

The creek will be developed for approximately six miles from State Line to the Blue River. When the creek project is completed, citizens will be able to boat in small boats on any one of nine bodies of water, hike on planned walking trails, or ride horseback along stretches of the waterway. The park board also hopes to see cafes and some other commercial activities develop along the banks. "We're even hoping," says Malyn, "because of the potential to be beside a beautiful lake in the Town Fork area, we can encourage residential redevelopment."

The Kansas City Zoo is home to a wide variety of rare and beautiful birds, some of them housed in the Tropical Habitat, which was the earliest zoo building.

CHAPTER XI

A Kingdom for Animals and People

ansas Citians have had a zoo in Swope Park almost as long as they have had Swope Park. For years, the two were so joined in the minds of citizens, that some (mostly relatives of Swope) raised a mild protest when the board voted in 1968 to change the name from Swope Park Zoo to Kansas City Zoo. But park commissioners insisted the zoo needed to be acknowledged as belonging to the entire community. This action undoubtedly helped in 1990, when voters city-wide, convinced that an improved Kansas City Zoo could benefit the entire community and attract nationwide attention, passed a $50 million bond issue for zoo renovation.

Interest in a zoo dates to 1907 when the Kansas City Zoological Society was formed and W.V. Lippencott named president. The next year, the society asked the Board of Park Commissioners for a zoo site in Swope Park. The board set aside sixty acres and allocated $32,000 to build the main zoo building, dedicated December 1909.

According to the city charter, the park board became responsible for the zoo because it was on park property. But the Zoological Society felt it knew more "about wild animals and their fancies." The board compromised by asking the society to act in an advisory capacity. To this day, no other city as large as Kansas City manages its zoo.

During the first ten years, the zoo was little more than a collection of barnyard animals given by individuals. To these were added a few "jungle-type" animals (three lions, some monkeys and a bear) bought from a dying circus. The zoo also obtained a grizzly bear from Yellowstone National Park. On a summer day in 1914, shortly after his arrival, the bear escaped by climbing a fourteen-foot-high stone wall and pushing himself through iron bars surrounding the zoo. During the next two weeks, the bear was spotted at several different places near Swope Park, and as far as thirty-five miles away, causing residents considerable worry. He was finally corralled and killed at Mount Washington Cemetery.

In 1919, Norman "Tex" Clark, who operated circus menageries, became the zoo's first fulltime manager. Under Clark's direction, the zoo acquired a more representative collection of birds and animals.

Individuals and civic organizations continued to give the zoo valuable gifts, the most famous of which were two elephants, Ararat and Temple, from the Ararat Shrine Temple. The zoo received another unique gift in March 1953 — three European white storks donated by Crawford's Blessed Event Dress Shop.

When Clark died in 1942, the park board conducted a national search for a new director and found William T.A. Cully at the Bronx Zoo in New York City. Cully brought twenty-five years of experience as a zoo specialist to his new job, and the zoo began to expand significantly. In 1948, the zoo opened its popular Children's Zoo featuring domestic animals (just right for petting) and a miniature train. Some years later, Hallmark Cards, Inc. made the Children's Zoo even more popular by adding the Birthday House where lively children could expend birthday party energy among the more docile animals.

A major modern attraction, the Seal Pool, was opened in May 1951. A concrete shelter in the center of a large outdoor circular pool houses sea lions who delight spectators by sunbathing on a kidney shaped island in the pool.

In 1964, the board dedicated another major modern attraction, the African Veldt, built on the site of an old stone quarry. The veldt allowed visitors to enjoy elephants, rhinos, red-necked ostriches, white bearded gnu, and other African animals in a more natural setting. The next year, the board approved a design for a building to house giraffes within the African Veldt. Other major attractions added to the zoo after 1954 were the Flamingo Pool, a bird house building, the Otter-Marina, The Great Ape House and The Great Cat Walk. Over recent years, there had been some small improvements but there hadn't been a major new exhibit in the zoo for over twenty years. Attendance also had been slowly decreasing and the community clearly knew that it was time to pass a major bond issue.

A chronic shortage of money, however, plagued the zoo from its

A NEW ZOO IDEA

During the early 1980s, Friends of the Zoo (FOTZ) wanted to do something that would really help a struggling Kansas City Zoo. FOTZ is a non-profit organization dedicated to the improvement and development of the zoo, by offering its membership educational services, wildlife conservation programs, the award-winning *ZOOmin'* magazine and **FRIENDS** newsletters and special events such as the annual FOTZ picnic.

However, by 1984, membership had dwindled to under 900. According to Anita Gorman, "Jerry Darter [park director] and I met with Sandy Berkley and said 'something's got to happen.' She took over FOTZ and in two years built it to over 7,000 members. I can never laud her enough."

Members of the organization wanted to do something about educating zoo visitors but rejected a traditional building with meeting rooms and classrooms and a theater. The Friends of the Zoo wanted something different.

To explore ideas, FOTZ and interested citizens formed a planning committee. In 1988, committee members, including the new park director Terry Dopson and deputy director Mark McHenry, went to Florida to study Epcot and Disney World. "That was when they first realized that what you to do is immerse the visitor in the experience," says Al Mauro, FOTZ president.

The ideas that arose in FOTZ planning committee meetings fit well with the environmental concerns of zoo supporters and the general public. The community at large is eagerly awaiting a changed zoo. Al Mauro says, "We were able to convince the public that this is a noble cause."

As the new zoo is developed, the beautiful Winged Waterways exhibit will remain as a habitat for many species of waterfowl.

formation and kept dreams unrealized. When the board hired Ralph Waterhouse as the zoo director in 1987, it asked him to renovate the entire zoo in a large chunk rather than in small increments. Other changes followed soon after. Upon the retirement of Jerry Darter, the board hired Terry Dopson as director in January, 1988. With Waterhouse and Dopson to lead the staff effort, the board turned to Jack Craft to chair the campaign and to the community for support, organizations — most notably the Friends of the Zoo and the Zoo docents — as well as businesses. Civic groups, even schools, worked in the "New Zoo" campaign. Overwhelmingly, voters passed the zoo bonds in 1990.

"The community spoke out loud and clear," Waterhouse says. "They wanted a better zoo." Deputy Park Director Mark McHenry, who has been assigned by Dopson to manage the new zoo project, says he believes the success of the zoo bond drive was due to the involvement of a lot of special interest groups. "I think dealing with all those interested parties, working in harmony with them and bringing them in early so they were part of the planning process was the reason for the success. They became married to it. It was not us and them. We were all in it together."

Implementation of the first phase of construction on the zoo master plan will begin in 1991 with the expectation that exhibits will open to the public by 1994 or early 1995.

The renovation of the zoo and the accompanying changes at Swope Park constitute the largest project undertaken by the park board since its beginning a hundred years ago. "The new zoo won't happen overnight. You have to go back to when Kessler first laid out his plans for the boulevard system to see anything comparable," says Mike Herron, park boulevard manager, "and realize it took Kessler some years to achieve the essence of that plan."

In addition to changes in the exhibition of animals, the new zoo will include the "Kingdom of the Animals," an education and orientation complex at the zoo entrance. The Friends of the Zoo is raising $16 million for the project.

A new concept in zoo education and public entertainment, the complex will be the center of wildlife and environmental education for the entire midwest. "The educational mission is the highest reason for the existence of the new zoo," says Waterhouse, who believes visitors need to be reached on an emotional level so they can appreciate the concerns environmentalists have for our planet. Zoos play a special role in this educational process, he says. "If we can protect and preserve the animals of the world, we'll protect and preserve the habitat necessary for man to thrive and continue to survive."

For the new zoo, planners are taking the best from various zoos nationwide, as well as borrowing from Walt Disney whose idea was to take people out of their daily, humdrum lives into a world apart where they could experience again the awe and wonder they felt as children. The new zoo will transport visitors to places such as the plains of Africa, the forests of South America or the outback of Australia. It is planned to mimic nature and make visitors feel good about the way the animals live.

Sunsets in Swope Park are spectacular as the light shafts through the park's enormous trees.

CHAPTER XII

The Second Century

he park board's Second Century holds promise of wonderful projects as yet only scarcely imagined. But some projects are already in planning. At least one major improvement will occur in three different parks, each representing a Missouri county in the Kansas City park system: Swope Park in Jackson County, Tiffany Springs Park in Platte County, and Hodge Park in Clay County.

"Swope will always be our Number One park," said board president Anita Gorman in 1990 when the passage of the zoo bonds offered the opportunity for a number of other changes for the park as well.

"Five million dollars is going to be spent in Swope Park," says Mark McHenry, head of the zoo management team, "basic infrastructure improvements, road relocations, some shelter house relocations, athletic field improvements, work at the Lake of the Woods."

There will be more than physical improvements. A School of Horticulture is planned, financed in part by money from the annual Flower, Lawn and Garden Show, for some years a fundraising enterprise for the parks. Such a school has been long-time goal of the park board. "We have plans that we've been working on for over ten years," says Gorman. "We have seen the need for a School of Horticulture that will appeal to people who can go there and learn a good trade. We'll put the students to work. Everybody needs lawn care. I think it's a winning idea for us."

The board started to implement the zoo master plan in 1987 when it dedicated an administrative building named for Jerome Cohen, park commissioner from 1956 to 1963, who has been a part of the Friends of the Zoo since it began and has run the zoo picnic for more than thirty years.

A highly visible International Center and pavilion also is planned for Swope Park's Second Century. Organized by Carl DiCapo, park commissioner, the annual three-day Ethnic Festival held in the park is an eagerly anticipated public event.

Tiffany Springs Park, located just south of the Kansas City International Airport, is scheduled to have a new golf course. "It takes a while to make a golf course, but we should have it by the end of the century," says Gorman who explains the course will be unusual because part of its location is on the site of a quarry. "That will be unique for Kansas City's parks system. We may have the only golf course in the country with a quarry." A small conference center is also part of future plans because of Tiffany Springs' proximity to the airport.

Hodge Park is scheduled to have an unusual shelter house to accommodate big groups. "We don't have a shelter worthy of the name north of the river," says Gorman. "We have small ones for families, but when Ford Motor Company or a large church wants to have a gathering they have to go somewhere else." The innovative shelter itself will be in the middle of a lake. A natural amphitheater that will hold up to 2,000 on the shore of the lake will seat audiences for concerts and other performances.

❧

The City Within a Park

For the urban dweller, trees are lifegiving in both a real and a symbolic sense. The green, leafy branches of tall trees are protective barriers against heat and wind, particularly during the summer months. Trees in the city represent the emotional opportunity to reach beneath the concrete and asphalt and plant spiritual roots in nature's soil.

As scientists and planners look ahead to discover ways for mankind to care for the planet, a study of places is emerging that explores how people live in relation to their environments. A recent survey of children all over the world asked for a list of things they needed to be happy. Children everywhere listed trees first, even — most astonishingly — in areas such as the Arctic Circle where trees are not part of the landscape. Primal in

Tiffany Springs Park located in Platte County south of the Kansas City International Airport will figure prominently in development plans for the park board's Second Century. The park will have a golf course and a small convention center.

In acknowledgement of twelve years of service and leadership by Anita B. Gorman, to the parks, the board named the park at North Oak Street and Vivion Road for her. Ollie Gates, named president of the board in 1991, presided at the dedication ceremonies.

Before being purchased by the park board in 1984, the Flower, Lawn & Garden Show was owned successively by three different entrepreneurs. The park board contracted each year with two of these independent owners, providing a special feature garden for their shows. In the past seven years, under George Eib's direction, the show has expanded and become increasingly successful financially. Each year the show has a different theme but Eib stresses gardening education every year. "We always want people to get ideas for their own yards," he says.

the human animal and pervasive among people everywhere, researchers concluded, is the hunger for trees.

Kessler and Meyer knew this need. They understood that modern man was destined to live within cities, but they believed it was desirable to live in a "city within a park," surrounded by daily reminders of pastoral serenity.

"In the nature of every human being," Kessler wrote in 1892, "is inherent a desire for the enjoyment of rural scenes, and what man or woman does not feel the elevating influences of such surroundings after being caged within city walls for weeks or months! Since it is not possible for a large number of urban residents to go out to the country, then as much as possible of its beauties should be brought within the city and made accessible to all."

Whatever else Kansas City has offered its residents and visitors, since its beginning it has boasted magnificent trees and green spaces. In a July 13, 1965 editorial, the *Kansas City Star* remarked on the impressions of first-time visitors to the city. "They seem to expect a dust bowl on the rim of the prairie," the *Star* wrote. "Instead they find a city, set in a forest."

"When people think of Kansas City, they think of trees, they think of greenery," says Michael Herron, park staff coordinator with the Kessler Society. "When they ask 'How did Kansas City get all this?' we tell them about George Kessler."

In 1990, the park board helped establish a citizen support organization, The Kessler Society, to help maintain, beautify and extend the miles of boulevards and the park system. Named, of course, for George Kessler, the society is dedicated to the creation of a "city within a park."

According to Herron, "People often join the Society so they can learn and implement changes in their own areas. It's a revitalizing of the City Beautiful movement."

The Kessler Society also attracts membership from the many other cities where Kessler planned parks and boulevards. "We've had just as much interest displayed in the Kessler Society from people living outside the Kansas City area as those living here," Herron says. In addition, engineers, landscape architects, urban planners, and architects who have come to appreciate Kessler's work support the Kessler Society. "The Kessler Society is up and going," says Commissioner Ollie Gates, "and it is going to be one of the nicest things that ever happened to Kansas City."

No one knows how August Meyer and George Kessler envisioned their plans being actualized, but implementing the 1893 Plan

meant involving Kansas Citians in a host of matters. Whose land would be taken? Whose taxes would pay for it? What would be the scope and impact of the plan?

This interactive planning process continues today. As soon as the park board publishes a plan, people react to it, favorably or unfavorably, and these reactions eventually affect final implementation.

To celebrate the Second Century, a development committee, under the leadership of park commissioner Ollie Gates and Hallmark executive Robert Kipp, searched for a project that would symbolize the spirit of participation by all citizens.

"What the Second Century idea is all about is to try to capture that spirit of participation," Kipp says. He believes the community must have vision and leadership that say, let's not get so caught up in the day-to-day that we lose sight of the longer term.

The committee ultimately decided on a Centennial Boulevard to link the entire city and revitalize older areas — forty miles of natural beauty between Tiffany Springs Park, south of the airport, and Jerry Smith Park at Prospect Avenue and 135th Street. According to Mike Herron, "If you look at the system we have, it represents what Kessler had in mind but we haven't extended beyond his vision with our annexations in either the north or the south."

The committee invited three major engineering/architectural firms, Black & Veatch, Burns & McDonnell, and Howard Needles Tammen & Bergendoff, to share their landscape architects' services in planning the boulevard route, and they all agreed.

The proposed boulevard will start at Tiffany Springs Park south of the airport, connect to the existing section of the Tiffany Springs Parkway and a proposed Line Creek Parkway before turning south and east. To cross the Missouri River, the committee believes a new Chouteau Bridge will need to be constructed to boulevard standards. After tying into Riverfront Road south of the river, the traffic will move over the existing Chestnut Trafficway and Independence Boulevard to The Paseo, then onto Meyer and Swope Parkway boulevards. A planned extension will connect with Gregory Boulevard and carry traffic through Swope Park to Blue River Road, then south to Jerry Smith Park.

"We'll start with Line Creek Parkway," Dopson says, "and probably do only one mile from Barry Road to Stagecoach, but that will be the first step of a Centennial Boulevard that will last 100 years."

According to Herron, Centennial Boulevard is expected to unite neighbors, not divide them. "The Paseo corridor will offer an oppor-

AN ETHNIC CENTER AT SWOPE PARK

One of the features in the master plan for an expanded Swope Park is an International Center that would function as a home for the many ethnic groups represented in Kansas City's population. The Center is a dream of Park Commissioner Carl DiCapo, restauranteur, chairman of the board of Italian Gardens, creator of the Ethnic Enrichment Club, and a principal supporter of all ethnic festivals held throughout the year in the city.

It all started in 1975, DiCapo says, when "Mayor Wheeler appointed me chairman of the Bicentennial. Having no idea what we were to do, he said that in the east they had an ethnic type observance where they did food. With my being in the restaurant business, I felt that would be a logical thing, and that's what we did. We got approximately twenty-two ethnic groups together, and we decided on an Ethnic Enrichment Club that would do things that would show people how all of us are the same, but with some terrific differences."

During each month of the Bicentennial year, DiCapo says, members from various ethnic groups visited schools to talk to students about their heritage, with emphasis on the kind of clothes worn, the food eaten, the games played, and anything else peculiar to their ethnic culture. "Then we did an overview of each of the ethnic groups, how they came into Kansas City, where they came from, what first led them here and how they were distributed.

After the Bicentennial, the group continued to meet and decided to have a festival at the Liberty Memorial. With the help of the park department and with almost no public notice, the festival attracted 5,000 people.

The properly impressed mayor made the Ethnic Club a commission with a representative of each ethnic group on a governing board. Since that time the commission has grown to represent fifty different cultures.

"We had such a great relationship with the park board, we asked them if we could be under their management," DiCapo says. In addition to the individual celebrations, the park board helps the commission put on a major festival at Swope Park each year.

An International Center would focus the efforts of the group and the attention of the community. DiCapo said the master plan includes space for each ethnic group, a pavilion with amphitheater for performances and a "Versailles-type garden" that would be divided into different plots with each ethnic group invited to plant bushes, trees and flowers from their homelands.

The annual Ethnic Festival brings out the city's most colorful dance troupes.

tunity to link a lot of ethnic and minority neighborhoods and take what is probably the most historically significant boulevard within the system and incorporate it within the idea of the Centennial Boulevard. We have landscape plans already developed for enhancement of The Paseo, retaining what we have left out of the original design and trying to improve upon what Kessler gave us."

According to Commissioner Gates, "We will use The Paseo as the vertebrae for our system. All the roads branching off will tie our city together as it becomes one great big greenway rather than all these different ethnic areas. Boulevards are created for leisure driving to allow everybody to understand, to see how everybody lives, and see how they interact with each other — so we can all feel comfortable."

Kipp agrees with Gates' vision. "If we could realize that dream," he says, "we could cause people to come together around it. They could experience the fact that while there's a river between north and south, bridges can get across the river, and while people with white skin and black skin look different, they aspire to the same things. The plans for this dream are there. All we have to do is extract them and excite the people about them."

Landscape architects visualize Centennial Boulevard as a significant spoke in two concentric wheels that would one day encircle the entire metropolitan area, preserve the natural landscape and its historic features, and provide recreational and cultural advantages for area residents and visitors. This dream of expanding George Kessler's "Kansas City only" park and boulevard system to the entire metropolitan community has taken shape as the Community Assistance Team Project of the Prairie Gateway Chapter of the American Society of Landscape Architects (ASLA) prepared a celebration of the ASLA 1991 national meeting in Kansas City.

In cooperation with representatives of more than eighty-five local parks and planning jurisdictions and the Mid-America Regional Council, the landscape architects studied the five urban counties (Clay, Jackson, Johnson, Platte, and Wyandotte) and completed comprehensive inventories of land forms, land use, vegetation, and transportation patterns, as well as existing recreational and cultural features. Their plan offers the diverse metropolitan community an integrated system of parks, parkways and water courses, and a unifying framework for the development of residential and commercial growth.

The inner circle of the metropolitan greenway system would loosely follow the route of I-435 which now encircles the city. At its northern extremities, the much larger outer circle would turn east several miles beyond the junction of I-435 and I-29 and go to the limits of Clay County; then turn south toward Independence, Raytown and Lee's Summit all the way to the Jackson County line before turning west along 175th Street in Johnson County toward Gardner, Kansas; then north to the Wyandotte County line, and into Platte County.

A major concern of the planners of this greenway system, as well as those planning the Centennial Boulevard, is unity for the metro area's diverse populations.

A system of graceful boulevards, spacious parks and beautiful fountains helped give Kansas City its lasting character. Successive boards of park commissioners have followed faithfully the early vision that foresaw the importance of a green legacy for generations to come. Today 187 parks comprising 10,027 acres of parkland; 165 miles of parkway and boulevards; 33 public fountains; and 47 monuments distinguish Kansas City from every other city in America. No other city is so blessed.

In the Second Century, the park board will continue to build on this legacy and to shore up a crucial sense of community. The Paseo, restored to its original grandeur, will link Tiffany Springs Park, the International Airport and the Northland to the people and spaces of south Kansas City.

In the same way, a new Brush Creek with its water walk will unite the ambience of The Plaza and the Nelson-Atkins Museum of Art with the vitality of the Bruce R. Watkins Cultural Heritage Center. Just as the eccentricities of topography once excited Kessler and other landscape planners, the texture of city life drawn from many cultures will serve to stimulate creative ideas about urban living in the century to come.

Because of a worldwide awakening to the plight of this endangered planet, it seems likely that ideas about city living will center on conservation and celebration of natural resources. Then, more than ever, Kansas City will glory in being a city within a park.

EPILOGUE

Kansas City at the close of the nineteenth century was a community of extravagant hopes located in a setting of squalid vitality. In the 1890s some of its leading citizens chose to create a park system to improve the quality of life here and remold the city's image.

Our city is fortunate to have a tradition of competent people applying themselves to work on the parks system with sustained and practical vision. The elements of a park can be found in virtually any settlement: plants, paving and walls. It is the arrangement, development, preservation and maintenance of these that distinguishes our city.

Kansas City can now take admirable pride in its parks system. Our appreciation of our legacy of parks and boulevards is increased still more when we consider their achievement from the perspective of the founders of the Parks Commission, a century ago.

Progress was the spirit which inspired men such as Nelson, Meyer, Kessler and Haff in their work instigating Kansas City's parks system. These boosters were pragmatic men who promoted parks as a means for basic city planning and economic development.

They used the parks system to drive the city forward, building an extraordinary, vital and sophisticated setting for what was previously a very ordinary settlement.

The parks and boulevards became the city's bones, providing structure and guidance for future development. There was much attention to exploiting interesting topographical features and using local materials, especially native limestone. Kessler's plans for a system of interconnecting boulevards became a planning tool which gave agreeable and natural form and measure to both residential and commercial developments.

Kansas City's tradition of parks and boulevards established a standard which informed the sensibilities of planners and citizens of all communities in the metropolitan area. Kansas City must function as a regional city, for it is a single community economically.

At the time of this writing, Kansas City's 165 miles of boulevards traverse economically and ethnically diverse districts within its boundaries. In all instances, the effect has been not only to improve the aesthetics, but also to raise the standards of maintenance and general quality of adjacent neighborhoods. Most modern roads do not perform this so well as our park-like boulevards.

The parks have also become the city's playground. A century ago, there was little recognition of the need for public recreation in the parks system. Organized sports, a more democratic spirit and the realization that fresh air and fitness go together have linked recreation to the parks system.

The city planners and landscape architects who laid out the parks and boulevards were clearly addressing the human need for contact with nature. The parks were intended to open up congested areas, to reduce concentrated development. The character of the boulevards system was incorporated in surrounding residential developments, so that in many cases the transition between public and private spaces is seamless and elegant.

The parks and boulevards are a mirror reflecting the images of the community. These are some of what we see in our parks: A city which anticipates growth. A city which provides first class recreational facilities for common citizens. A city which considers natural beauty to be an important component to modern urban life.

The Parks Commissioners have been conscientious stewards, carefully guarding the heritage of the Kansas City's parks with the certain knowledge that they are owned not by the Board, nor even by all the present citizens, but are held in trust for our children.

In our parks and gardens, nature provides for constant renewal; in our cities, we must take a more active role. As all Kansas Citians celebrate the first one hundred years of their parks system, considerable attention is being given to both expansion and integration of the system into suburbs and use of parks and boulevards to renew and revitalize the urban core. As always, such plans will be further shaped and tempered by politics, fiscal and other practical considerations. The fact is that we have in the parks system a model which works for the improvement of the quality of life in our city, is a basic tool for urban planning, and which reflects an image of ourselves as an attractive and considerate community.

As the city commemorates the Centenary of its Board of Parks Commissioners, we should look to the future, recognizing both the vision of our city's potential realized in the legacy of our parks, and the spirit of progress which still inspires us.

— *Jonathan Kemper*

KANSAS CITY PARKS

Admiral Plaza
Admiral Boulevard & Oak Street
Agnes Park
74th Street & Agnes Avenue
Arbor Villa Park
66th Street Terrace & Main Street
Arleta Park
77th Street & Prospect Avenue
Arno Park
Ward Parkway & 69th Street
Ashland Square
23rd Street & Elmwood Avenue
Bannister Park
9800 James A. Reed Road
Barry Road Park
7601 N.W. Barry Road
Belvidere Park
Independence Avenue
& Lydia Avenue
Bent Tree Park
98th Street & View High Drive
Big Shoal Greenway
Antioch Road to N. Brighton
Avenue, parallel to N. 56th Street
Blenheim Park
Gregory Boulevard & The Paseo
Blue Banks Park
4800 Colorado Avenue
Blue Hills Park
53rd Street & Brooklyn Avenue
Blue River Athletic Field
I-435 & Prospect Avenue
Blue Valley Park
23rd Street & Topping Avenue
Blue Valley Recreation Center
1801 White Avenue
Blues Park
20th Street & Prospect Avenue
Briarcliff Greenway
N.E. Barry Road & North
Garfield
Brookhill
N.E. 58th Street
& N. Jackson Avenue
Brooklyn Park
43rd Street & Brooklyn Avenue
Brookside Court
Brookside Boulevard
& 56th Street
Sanford Brown Plaza
Linwood Boulevard
& Brooklyn Avenue

Buckeye Greenway
Mo. 210 & N. Brighton
to N. 37th Street
Budd Park
St. John Avenue
& Brighton Avenue
Ermine Case, Jr. Park
10th Street & Jefferson Street
Cave Springs Park
7200 Westhavens Road
Central Park
Linwood Boulevard
& Bales Avenue
Chaumiere Woods Park
N. 43rd Street
& N. Indiana Avenue
Chelsea Park
26th Street & Chelsea Avenue
Chouteau Greenway
N. 38th Street to N. 43rd Street
Chouteau Park
N. 46th Street
& Chouteau Trafficway
City Hall Grounds
414 E. 12th Street
Clark-Ketterman Athletic Field
107th & Skiles Avenue
Clayton Park
N.E. 64th Terrace
& N. Belleview Street
Cleveland Park
43rd Street & Cleveland Avenue
Columbus Square
Missouri Avenue & Holmes Street
Commonwealth Green
Gillham Road
& Armour Boulevard
Cooley Park
N. Antioch Road & Winn Road
Corrington Park
18th Street & Corrington Avenue
Crestview Park
N. 43rd Street
& N. Troost Avenue
Nelson C. Crews Square
27th Street & Woodland Avenue
Cypress Park
29th Street & Cypress Avenue
Jerry Darter Park
105th Street & Hillcrest Road
Davidson Park
N. 53rd Street
& N. Woodland Avenue

Murray Davis Park
40th Street & Main Street
Douglas Park
2632 Jarboe Street
Andrew Drips Park
16th Street & Belleview Street
Dunbar Park
36th Street & Oakley Avenue
Wilbur H. Dunn Park
The Paseo & Meyer Boulevard
Eastwood Park
Sni-A-Bar Road
& Bennington Avenue
Englewood Park
N.E. Englewood Road
& N. Troost Avenue
Ewing Park
107th Street & Ewing Avenue
Fairview Park
38th Terrace & Arlington Avenue
Fox Hill Park
N.E. 104th Street & Cherry Drive
Freeway Park
14th Street & Indiana Avenue
French Tract
Bannister (95th Street) to 99th on
East side of K.C. So. R.R.
Gage Park
23rd Street & Jarboe Street
Gambril Tract
108th Street &
St. Catherines Lane
Garrison Square
5th Street & Troost Avenue
Robert Gillham Park
Gillham Road & 42nd Street
Golden Oaks Park
N.E. 46th Street
& N. Antioch Road
Anita B. Gorman Park
N.E. 46th Street Terrace & Davidson
Road and North Oak & Vivion Road
Green Hills Park
Green Hills Road & Bryan Avenue
Harmony Park
10th Street & Agnes Avenue
Hawthorne Park
Gillham Road & 27th Street
Heim Park
Chestnut Trafficway
& Martin Avenue
Hibbs Park
59th Street & Spruce Avenue

Hidden Valley Park
N.E. Russell Road
& N. Bennington Avenue
Highland View Park
N.E. 85th Terrace
& Virginia Avenue
Robert H. Hodge Park
7000 N.E. Barry Road
Holmes Park
69th Street & Holmes Road
Hospital Hill Park
Gillham Road & 22nd Street
Hyde Park
Gillham Road & 38th Street
Independence Plaza
Independence Boulevard
& Park Avenue
Indian Creek Greenway
103rd Street & Wornall Road
Indian Mound
Gladstone Boulevard
& Belmont Boulevard
Indiana Park
25th Street & Indiana Avenue
Ingles Park
118th Street & Bristol Avenue
Iser Park
112th Terrace
& Sycamore Avenue
Jarboe Park
17th Street & Jarboe Street
Margaret Kemp Park
10th Street & Harrison Street
Kemper Arena Grounds
1800 Genessee Street
George E. Kessler Park
The Paseo to Belmont Boulevard,
North Bluffs
Thomas J. Kiely Park
The Paseo & 47th Street
Martin Luther King, Jr. Square
Swope Parkway
& Woodland Avenue
Kirby Creek Park
N.E. 81st Street
& Woodland Avenue
Klapmeyer Park
126th Street & State Line
Lakewood Greenway
I-35 to N.E. Vivion Road parallel
to N. Norton Avenue
Legacy East Park
91st Street & Brooklyn Avenue

KANSAS CITY PARKS

Legacy West Preserve
94th Street & Troost Avenue

Liberty Park
34th Terrace & Stadium Drive

Linwood Green
Linwood Boulevard & Lister Avenue
to Poplar Avenue

Longfellow Park
Gillham Road & 25th Street

Jacob L. Loose Park
51st Street & Wornall Road

Johnston E. Lykins Square
8th Street & Myrtle Avenue

Manheim Green
Manheim Road & 40th Street

Maple Park
Maple Boulevard
& Lexington Avenue

Marlborough Park
83rd Street & Park Avenue

Carl Migliazzo Park
Minor Drive
& Pennsylvania Avenue

Mill Creek Park
J.C. Nichols Parkway & 43rd Street
to Ward Parkway

William Minor Park
Red Bridge Road (111th Street)
& Holmes Road

Montgall Park
22nd Street & Agnes Avenue

Morgan Tract
5800 N. Broadway

Mulkey Square
13th Street & Summit Street

Nelson-Atkins Museum of Art Grounds
Brush Creek Boulevard
& Oak Street

Nicholson Ball Diamond
3601 East Nicholson Avenue

Noble Park
75th Street & Cleveland Avenue

North Congress Greenway
N.W. 68th Street & Mace Road

North Hills Park
So. of N. 36th Street & West of I-29
& I-35

Northeast Athletic Field
6500 East St. John Avenue

Northwood Park
N.W. 56th Street west of
Northwood Road

Oak Park
43rd Street & Agnes Avenue

Observation Park
20th Street & Holly Street

Satchel Paige Stadium
5200 East 51st Street

Palmer Park
53rd Street & Smalley Avenue

Park Forest
N.W. 73rd Street
& N. Autumn Avenue

Paseo Green
The Paseo, 9th & 12th Sts.

Penn Valley Park
Pershing Road & Main Street

Platte Brooke North
N.W. Platte Brooke Drive
& North Grandby

Pioneer Park
Broadway & Westport Road

Prather Park
Parvin Road & Prather Road

Prospect Plaza Park
12th Street & Prospect Avenue

Raytown Road Athletic Field
Eastern Trafficway
& Raytown Road

James A. Reed Park
89th Street & James A. Reed Road

Riverfront Park
River Front Road
& N. Monroe Avenue

Riverview Greenway
N. 32nd Street & Holmes Road
Northeasterly to Russell Road

Roanoke Park
Valentine Road to 34th Street
& Karnes Boulevard

Roanoke Plaza
Roanoke Parkway & 47th Street

Robinhood Park
N.W. 72nd Street
& Robinhood Lane

Rock Creek Park
Byers Avenue & Antioch Road

Romey Hills Park
N.E. 101st Place & N. Main Street

Ruskin Way Park
114th Street & Ruskin Way

Russell, Majors, Waddell Park
Ward Parkway & 83rd Street

Saeger Woods
135th Street & Woodland Avenue

San Rafael Park
N.E. 53rd Street & San Rafael Drive

Santa Fe Trace
117th Street & Holmes Road

Santa Fe Trail Park
23rd Street & Topping Avenue

Scott Park
4101 E. 100th Terrace

Seven Oaks Park
39th Street & Kensington Avenue

Sheffield Park
12th Street & Winchester Avenue

Sherrydale Park
N.E. 90th Terrace & N. Oak Street

Skiles Park
47th Street & Skiles Avenue

Jerry Smith Park
135th & Prospect Avenue

South Oak Park
83rd Street & Oak Street

Southmoreland Park
Brush Creek Boulevard
& Oak Street

Spring Valley Park and Plaza
27th Street & Woodland Avenue

Strathbury Park
I-29 & N.W. 60th Street

Sunnyside Park
83rd Street & Summit Street

Sunset Park
N. Garfield Avenue, N. 35th Street
to N. 34th Terrace

Thomas H. Swope Park
Swope Parkway
& Meyer Boulevard

Sycamore Knoll Park
Byfield Avenue No. of Barry Road

Sycamore Park
108th Street & Sycamore Avenue

Terrace Park
115th Street & Cleveland Avenue

The Concourse
Benton Boulevard & St. John Avenue

The Grove Park
Benton Boulevard & Truman Road

The Parade Park
The Paseo & Truman Road

Frank A. Theis Park
Brush Creek Boulevard & Oak Street

Tiffany Springs Park
N.W. 88th Street
& N.W. Hampton Road

Timber Valley Park
62nd Terrace & Marion Drive

Tower Park
76th Street & Holmes Road

Town Fork Creek Greenway
51st Street & Indiana Avenue
to 57th Street & Agnes Avenue

Lafayette Traber Garden
Woodland Avenue
& Pendleton Street

Troost Park
The Paseo & 31st Street

Union Cemetery
Warwick Boulevard & 28th Street

Van Brunt Park
Van Brunt Boulevard
& 16th Street

Frank Vaydik-Line Creek Park
N.W. 56th Street
& N.W. Waukomis Drive

Vineyard Park
40th Terrace & Vineyard Drive

Warford Park
114th Street & Cleveland Avenue

Washington Square Park
Pershing Road & Grand Avenue

Water Works Park
3200 N. Oak Trafficway

West Pennway Park
20th Street & Madison Street

West Rock Creek Park
27th Street & Hunter Avenue

West Terrace Park
West Bluffs, 6th Street to 17th Street

Westwood Park
47th Street & Wyoming Street

White Oak Park
89th Street & Crescent Avenue

Wildberry Park
N.W. 87th Street & Pomona Avenue

Winner Park
8400 E. Independence Avenue

Winnwood Park
N. 44th Street
& N. Cypress Avenue

Woodgate Park
97th Street & Elm Avenue

Woodsmoke Park
N.W. 70th Street & Hilldale

KANSAS CITY BOULEVARDS AND PARKWAYS

29th Street
Wyandotte Street to Broadway

38th Street Boulevard
Broadway (400W)
to Roanoke Road (1200W)

40th Street Manheim
From Virginia Avenue
to The Paseo (1 block)

Admiral Boulevard
Grand Avenue (200E)
to Highland Avenue (1700E)

Armour Boulevard
Broadway (400W)
to The Paseo (1400E)

Belmont Boulevard
Street John Avenue (100S)
to Swope Parkway (4900S)
Benton Plaza 0.26 miles included
in Benton Boulevard

Blue River Road
Oldham Road to southwest limit
of Swope Park

Boat House Road
Riverside Road between Polo
Ground and Boat House
to Riverside Road

Broadway
26th Street to 43rd Street
(not including Penn Valley R/W)

Brookside Boulevard
48th and Main Street
to Meyer Boulevard (6400S)

Brush Creek Boulevard
J.C. Nichols Parkway to The Paseo
and on to Elmwood Avenue

Cliff Drive
The Paseo north
to Gladstone Boulevard

Gladstone Boulevard
Independence Avenue north and
east to Belmont Avenue (6200E)

Gregory Boulevard
From Ward Parkway (1100W)
to Elmwood Avenue

Harrison Boulevard
Armour Boulevard (3500S)
to 39th Street

Harrison Parkway
Gillham Road & 39th Street
northeast to Harrison Boulevard

Highland Avenue
Independence Boulevard
to Admiral Boulevard (1 block)

Hillcrest Road
Oldham Road to south limits
of Swope Park

Holmes Road
Rockhill Road at 66th Terr.
to a point 180 ft. south of the
center line of 77th Street

Independence Boulevard
Highland Avenue (1700E)
to Benton Boulevard (3200E)

Karnes Boulevard
Pennsylvania Street (600W)
at 31st Street
to Roanoke Road (1200W)

Kessler Road
Pershing Road (200W) south
to Pioneer Mother Drive (300W)

Lakeside Drive
Gregory Boulevard north to 67th
& Lewis Road

Lewis Road
Lakeside Drive north
to 63rd Street Trafficway

Linwood Boulevard
Van Brunt Boulevard (5400E)
to Main Street

Manheim Road
The Paseo north to Holmes Street
(700E)

Maple Boulevard
Independence Avenue (600S)
to Missouri Avenue (500S)

Meyer Boulevard
Ward Parkway (1100W)
to Swope Parkway (3800E)

Oakwood Drive
Oldham Road to Oakwood road

Oakwood Road
Oakwood Drive to Oldham Road

Oldham Road
Gregory Boulevard to south limits
of Swope Park

Pavilion Road
A loop off Starlight Road

Penn Valley Place
Pennsylvania Avenue
to Pennsylvania Drive

Pennsylvania Drive
Pennsylvania Avenue to 27th Street

Prospect Boulevard
Independence Boulevard (600S)
north to Lexington Avenue (300S)

Red Bridge Road
Wornall Rd. to Blue River Road

Riverside Road
Lakeside Drive to Lewis Road

Roanoke Boulevard
Karnes Boulevard to Valentine Road

Rockhill Road
Gregory Boulevard (7100S)
north to 45th Street

Rockhill Terrace
Brush Creek Boulevard north
and west to West Gillham Road

Spring Valley Drive
27th Street to 29th Street

Starlight Road
Swope Parkway to Zoo Drive

Swope Memorial Drive
From Gregory Boulevard to
Swope Memorial Clubhouse

The Mall Drive
Starlight Road to Zoo Drive

Troost Lake Drive
The Paseo to Vine Street

Valentine Road
Broadway (400W) west to
Genessee Street (1700W)

Van Brunt Boulevard
Gladstone Boulevard (500N)
south and southwest to
Elmwood Avenue (4500S)

Volker Boulevard
Brookside Boulevard (200E)
to The Paseo (1400E)

Warwick Boulevard
Linwood Boulevard (3200S)
to Brush Creek Boulevard (4700S)

West Paseo Boulevard
24th Street to 27th Street

Wildcat Hollow Drive
Lakeside Drive (67th Street)
to east limits of Swope Park

Zoo Drive
Gregory Boulevard
to Starlight parking lot and
from Starlight parking lot
to 63rd Street Trafficway

KANSAS CITY FOUNTAINS AND MONUMENTS

FOUNTAINS

49/63 Neighborhood Fountain
The Paseo and Lydia Avenue

9th Street Fountain
The Paseo and 9th Street

American War Mothers Memorial
Meyer Boulevard and The Paseo

Columbus Square Fountain
Missouri Avenue and Holmes Street
(Columbus Square Park)

Eagle Scout Memorial
Gillham Road at 39th Street

Robert Gillham Fountain
Gillham Road and 42nd Street

Delbert J. Haff Circle Fountain
Meyer Boulevard and
Swope Parkway

Heritage Fountain
2400 Beacon Avenue (Blue Valley Park)

Liberty Memorial Fountain
North entrance to memorial below
the Great Frieze (Penn Valley Park)

Loose Park Rose Garden Fountain
South of entrance on east side of
park in the lake (Jacob L. Loose Park)

Harry Evans Minty Memorial Fountain
Within the Great Cat Walk Exhibit
(Kansas City Zoo)

Mirror Pool
Ward Parkway and 61st Street

Muse of the Missouri
8th Street and Main St.

J.C. Nichols Memorial Fountain
Between J.C. Nichols Parkway and
Main Street on 47th Street
(Mill Creek Park)

Northland Fountain
No. Oak Street and No. Vivion Rd.
(Northgate Park)

Bernard Powell Memorial Fountain
28th Street and Brooklyn Avenue
(Spring Valley Park)

Prospect Plaza Fountain
11th Street and Prospect Avenue

Romany Fountain
Ward Parkway and Romany Dr.

Sea Horse Fountain
Meyer Boulevard and
Ward Parkway (Meyer Circle)

Seville Light Fountain
J.C. Nichols Parkway on a traffic
island at the northwest corner
of 47th Street

Sittenfeld Memorial Fountain
Near Cheetah Compound (KC Zoo)

Spirit of Freedom Fountain
Brush Creek Boulevard and
Cleveland Avenue

Thomas H. Swope Memorial Fountain
West of Thomas H. Swope
Memorial (Kessler Park)

Vietnam Memorial Fountain
Broadway and 42nd Street

William Volker Memorial Fountain
Volker Boulevard and Oak Street
(Frank Theis Park)

Fountain
The Paseo and 79th Street

Fountain
Ward Parkway and 69th Street

MONUMENTS

American Legion Memorial I
Budd Park Esplanade, east side
of Van Brunt Boulevard

American Legion Memorial II
Meyer Boulevard entrance to
Swope Park, north of Loose
Memorial Flag Pole

Army Mothers' Founders Post
(United States) Memorial
West side of the Mall in center of
tree grove (Penn Valley Park)

Battle of Westport Monument
North of Rose Garden adjacent to
52nd Street (Jacob L. Loose Park)

**Battle of Westport Grand Army of the
Republic Monument**
The Paseo and 63rd Street

Alfred Benjamin Memorial
Starlight Road and Pavilion Road
southeast of band pavilion
(Swope Park)

Thomas Hart Benton Memorial
Intersection of Gladstone and
Benton Boulevards and St. John
Avenue (Kessler Park)

William J. Bland Memorial
East side of Gillham Road
and 42nd Street

Murray Davis Memorial
On an island at Main and 40th Sts.

N. Clyde Degginger Memorial
"Sheep Piece" North of Brush Creek
Boulevard and east of gallery walks
(The Nelson-Atkins Museum of Art)

Andrew Drips Monument
North side of 16th Street between
Jarboe Street and Belleview Avenue
(Andrew Drips Park)

The Eagle Monument
Ward Parkway and 70th Street

89th Division Memorial
Flag Pole at South entrance to Liberty
Memorial Mall (Penn Valley Park)

William T. Fitzsimmons Memorial
The Paseo and 12th Street

Fitzsimmons-Battenfeld Monument
The Paseo on north side of triangle at
47th Street (Kiely Park)

Mary A. Fraser Memorial
Next to Sea Lion Pool (K. C. Zoo)

Salvatore Grisafe Memorial
The Paseo median at 16th Street

Delbert J. Haff Memorial
Meyer Boulevard and Monroe
Avenue west side of Pool

The Hiker Monument,
South of Liberty Memorial Mall
and Memorial Dr. (Penn Valley Park)

John F. Kennedy Memorial
Gladstone and Benton Boulevards
on the Concourse (Kessler Park)

Lewis and Clark Memorial
8th Street and Jefferson Street
overlooking the Missouri River
(West Terrace Park)

Liberty Memorial
Pershing Road and Main Street south
to Memorial Drive (Penn Valley Park)

Jacob L. Loose Memorial
East side of park, 51st Street and
Wornall Road (Jacob L. Loose Park)

Loose Memorial Flag Pole
Swope Parkway and Meyer Boulevard
Entrance east of Swope Interpretive
Center (Swope Park)

Massasoit Monument
J.C. Nichols Parkway on southeast
corner of 47th Street

August R. Meyer Memorial
The Paseo and 10th Street

**Meyer Circle Gateway Memorial —
Avenue of Trees**
Meyer Boulevard and Ward
Parkway south of fountain

Mormon Memorial
South of Troost Lake near 29th Street
(The Paseo)

**Navy Mothers' Club
(Heart of America) Memorial**
Stone bench east side of Mall
halfway down in grove of trees
(Penn Valley Park)

James Pendergast Memorial
13th Street and Madison Street
(Mulkey Square)

Pioneer Mother Memorial
Memorial Drive west of Street Mary's
Hospital (Penn Valley Park)

William R. Royster Memorial
Benton Boulevard and St. John
Avenue north of casting pool on The
Concourse (Kessler Park)

Santa Fe Trail Markers
Linwood Boulevard and Euclid Avenue
Gillham Road and 38th Street, South of
Liberty Memorial Mall
(Penn Valley Park) 27th Street and
Topping Street (Blue Valley Park)

Scarritt Point Memorial
West side of Walrond Street and
Norledge Avenue (Kessler Park)

The Scout
29th Street and Pennsylvania Street
overlooking Penn Valley Lake

Albert Elwood Shirling Sanctuary
South of west end of swinging bridge
at the Lagoon (Swope Park)

Karen Slack Memorial
South of 68th Street at The Paseo and
68th Street (Dunn Park)

Charles Carroll Spalding Memorial
South of Penn Valley Lake at 29th Street
and Pennsylvania Drive
(Penn Valley Park)

Spanish Cannon
The Paseo and 12th Street

Statue of Liberty
Meyer Boulevard and Prospect Avenue

Stone Lions
South side of City Hall
12th and Oak Streets

Thomas H. Swope Memorial
Northwest of Swope Memorial
Clubhouse on the summit of a hill
overlooking the Lagoon (Swope Park)

The Thinker Monument
44th Street at the north entrance to
the Nelson-Atkins Museum of Art

Union Cemetery Memorial
Warwick Trafficway and 28th Street

**United Daughters of the Confederacy
Memorial**
Ward Parkway and 55th Street

The Wagon Master
Ward Parkway, east bound,
just west of Wornall Road

George Washington Memorial
Pershing Road and Grand Avenue
(Washington Square Park)

Westport Memorial Marker
Broadway and 40th Street

KANSAS CITY PARK BOARD COMMISSIONERS

1892-1909

August R. Meyer, President	1892-1901
William C. Glass	1892-1895
S.B. Armour	1892-1899
Adriance Van Brunt	1892-1901
Louis Hammerslough	1892-1895
Charles Campbell	1895-1898
Robert Gillham	1895-1898
James Burnham	1898-1901
William Barton	1899-1901
J.V.C. Karnes	1899-1902
J.J. Swofford, President	1901-1905
J.F. Richards	1901-1905
Patrick Moore	1901-1905
C.J. Schmelzer	1901-1905
E.P. Neal	1901-1905
Franklin Hudson, President	1905-1909
Allen Dean	1905-1910
Fred S. Doggett	1905-1909
George W. Fuller	1905-1909
Robert L. Gregory	1905-1906
George T. Hall	1906-1909

Original board members responsible for 1893 Plan . . . Selling it to Kansas Citians . . . Construction started on The Paseo, North Terrace Park, Independence Plaza, Independence Blvd. and Holmes Square . . . Budd Park brought into the system . . . Legal battles.

Acquisition of Swope Park . . . work started on Penn Valley Park, The Grove, The Parade, Observation Park in West Terrace Park built . . . Passage of 1895 amendment vesting board with full responsibility for the park system.

Gift of Roanoke Park accepted . . . Gift of Southmoreland Park accepted from W.R. Nelson . . . Hyde Park created . . . Construction started on Gladstone Blvd. . . . Armour Blvd. . . . Spring Valley Park acquired . . . Work started on Gillham Road . . . Completion of original section of Benton Blvd. . . . Swope Park Zoo opened . . . Swope Parkway under construction . . . Garrison Square completed . . . Kessler report of 1910 stating original plan complete.

1910-1939

Delbert J. Haff, President		1909-1912
John W. Wagner		1909-1912
Henry D. Ashley, President	(1912-1913)	1910-1913
James E. Logan		1912-1915
Cusil Lechtman, President		1912-1916
		(1913-14,1915-16)
C.C. Carver, President	(1914-1915)	1913-1916
Shannon C. Douglass		1915-1916
George W. Fuller, President		1916-1918
Allen J. Dean, President		1916-1918
William Buchholz		1916-1920
Frank Sebree, President		1918-1922
Fred Huttig		1918-1924
Edwin W. Zea		1920-1926
Rollins M. Hockaday		1925-1927
Matthew A. Foster, President		1926-1930
Fred C. House		1926-1930
Elliott H. Jones		1927-1930
Joseph A. Guthrie, President		1930
Frank C. Niles		1930
David E. Long, President		1930-1936
L. Newton Wylder		1930-1933
Frank H. Cromwell, President	(1936-1938)	1930-1938
Robert E. Gees		1933-1940
Chester Cooke		1936-1938

Work started on Ward Parkway . . . Station Park accepted from railway terminal company . . . Washington Square completed . . . Mill Creek Parkway condemnation ordered . . . Van Brunt Blvd. named.

Meyer Blvd. and Rockhill Road construction started . . . Recreation Commission established . . . Land acquired for Karnes Blvd. . . . Plans for Blue Valley Parkway approved . . . Brookside Blvd. named . . . "The Scout" located in Penn Valley Park . . . First playground director hired . . . Swope Memorial plans approved . . . Brush Creek Parkway officially named and opened June 1917.

Pershing Road land condemned . . . Liberty Memorial land condemned . . . Warwick Blvd. brought into park system . . . land acquired for Chestnut Parkway and Linwood Blvd. . . . Board accepts gift of "Pioneer Mother."

Deed to Loose Park accepted on May 20, 1927 . . . Gregory Blvd. named . . . Rose garden for Loose Park approved.

Naming of Clark's Point . . . Dedication of W.H. Dunn Park . . . Board accepts Sea Horse fountain from J.C. Nichols.

1940-1963

James E. Nugent, President		1938-1940
William F. Newton		1938-1940
John A. Moore, President		1940-1948
H.H. Peters		1940-1942
Edwin R. Chandler		1940-1942
Harry E. Minty		1942-1948
Edward H. Glenn		1942-1947
Vincent H. Hagerty		1947-1952
J.J. Lynn		1944-1947
Claude Cochran		1947-1950
R. Carter Tucker, President		1948-1951
Frank A. Theis, President	(1952-1965)	1950-1965
Ned J. Fortney		1952-1955
Paul M. Fogel		1952-1955
George Fuller Green		1955-1959
John C. Monroe		1955-1956
Jerome Cohen		1956-1963
Wade D. Rubick		1959-1962
James Daleo		1962-1963

Part of Spring Valley Park named Nelson B. Crews Square . . . Board assumes responsibility for Kansas City Museum grounds.

Board negotiates new lease with War Dept. for rest camp in Penn Valley Park . . . Board agrees to maintain Union Cemetery but not to accept it as park property . . . Land selected for Bales Lake in what becomes Blue Valley Park . . . Nelson Art Gallery grounds accepted as park property . . . Moffat Tract addition to Swope Park approved . . . Plans approved for Starlight Theatre.

Andrew Drips monument approved . . . Volker Blvd. dedicated June 14, 1951 . . . Swope Park pool integrated by court order June 24, 1953 . . . Battle of Westport monument in Loose Park dedicated Oct. 23, 1953. . . Board approves sale of bonds for Northland parks and boulevards . . . African Veldt dedicated July 4, 1953 . . . Board passes resolution that all swimming and wading pools be integrated on May 18, 1955.

Land purchased for cultural mall south of the gallery . . . Minor Park land given . . . Board accepts contributions for J.C. Nichols fountain. . . Garden Center building at Loose Park complete . . . Volker Fountain dedicated Sept. 20, 1958 . . . Westport-Roanoke Community Center plans approved. Holmes Square sold . . . R. L. Sweet Arboretum dedicated May 6, 1961 . . . Board asks voters to approve a protection program for elms as result of Dutch elm disease . . . Board assumes joint control of Liberty Memorial with Liberty Memorial Association.

KANSAS CITY PARK BOARD COMMISSIONERS

1964-1978

Robert H. Hodge, M.D.	1963-1974
President	(1971-1974)
Lewis Dysart	1963-1971
Davis K. Jackson, President	1965-1971
Harold L. Holliday, Jr.	1971-1972
Carl Migliazzo	1971 1979
Jeremiah Cameron	1972-1979
Richard L. Marr, President	1974-1979

Recreation division merged with park board as result of voter approval of a charter change in November 1966 . . . Board accepts 385 acres of land purchased by city in Shoal Creek Park in Northland . . . Land at 63rd and Elmwood purchased for boulevard . . . Riverfront Park land acquired.

Plans approved for construction of Manchester Trafficway . . . More land added to Line Creek Park, Clark-Ketterman Athletic Field and Hidden Valley Park. . . John F. Kennedy memorial on Concourse in North Terrace Park approved . . . Eagle Scout memorial accepted . . . Tiffany Springs Park, second addition, authorized . . . also Indian Creek Park . . . Swope Park Zoo renamed Kansas City Zoo.

Linwood Multipurpose Center planned . . . James A. Reed park land acquired . . . Deed to land for Jerry Smith Park accepted . . . City of Fountains Foundation established . . . North Terrace renamed George Kessler Park . . . Shoal Creek Park named for Dr. Robert Hodge . . . Christo wraps the walks in Loose Park in saffron nylon . . . Heritage village in Hodge Park dedicated June 4, 1977 . . . Dutch elm disease brought under control.

1979-1992

L.P. Cookingham, President	1979-1986
LeeVertis Swinton	1979-1980
Anita Gorman, President (1986-1991)	1979-1991
Bruce Watkins	1980.
Ollie W. Gates	1980-
Carl DiCapo	1986
Sheila Kemper Dietrich	1991-

Outdoor Bronze Restoration Fund established . . . CYO Stadium restored and named for Satchel Paige . . . Flower, Lawn and Garden Show acquired by Board . . . Adopt a Park program begun . . . Spirit of Freedom Fountain dedicated . . . Carl Migliazzo Park dedicated . . . Volunteers in Parks program established . . . Northland Fountain dedicated . . . To aid parks, successful election raises levies and boulevard taxes for the first time since 1925 . . . Vietnam Memorial Fountain dedicated . . . Washington Square Park restored . . . 49-63 Fountain dedicated . . . Northland's Chaumiere Lake restored . . . Gillham Road reconstructed . . . Cliff Drive restored and waterfall fountain built . . . Significant public/private partnerships marked by various projects including dedications of Pioneer Park and sculptures, Mill Creek Park's Fitness Trails, and more than a dozen buildings reconstructed at historic Shoal Creek, Missouri . . . Dedication of Jerry Darter Park . . . Tiffany Springs Baseball Complex built . . . Bernard Powell Memorial dedicated . . . Swope Memorial Golf Course Clubhouse and Golf Course totally restored . . . Master plan for zoo completed and $50 million zoo bond election successful . . . Northland public pool facility secured through generosity of Raymond R. Brock, Jr. . . . Kessler Society formed . . . Three parks — Swope, Tiffany Springs and Hodge — designated for development to celebrate centennial . . . Anita B. Gorman Park dedicated . . . Rev. John Williams statue dedicated.

KANSAS CITY PARK BOARD DIRECTORS

W. H. Dunn
1904-1937

J. V. Lewis
1939-1963

Frank Vaydik
1964-1980

Jerry Darter
1980-1988

Terry Dopson
1988-

(Until 1964, directors were called park superintendents)

KANSAS CITY PARK BOARD SECRETARIES

Adriance Van Brunt
1892

George E. Kessler
1892-1902

John Ranson
1903

Alex R. Rankin
1904

F. P. Gossard
1905-1911

Thomas C. Harrington
1912-1916

W. T. Williams
1926-1930

Charles V. Garnett
1930-1931

Roger S. Miller
1931-1940

John C. Lacy
1940-1965

Richard E. Soper
1966-1988

Michael Herron
1988-

MAJOR SUPPORT GROUPS AND ASSOCIATIONS

Assistance League of Kansas City Northland
Audubon Society
Black & Veatch
Blue Cross Blue Shield
Boy Scouts of America
Burns & McDonnell Volunteers
Central Exchange
Chamber of Commerce of Greater Kansas City
Citizens Association-Board of Directors
City of Fountains Foundation
Civic Council of Greater Kansas City
Clay County Economic Development Council
Clay County Hotel/Motel Association
Clay/Platte Baseball Association
Commerce Bank of Kansas City Volunteers
Convention and Visitors Bureau of Greater Kansas City, Inc.
Crown Center Corporation Community
Dunn Construction
Eagle Scouts
Enrichment Commission
Ethnic Enrichment Commission, Gladstone Democratic Club
Friends of James Pendergast
Friends of Loose Park
Friends of Shoal Creek Association
Friends of the Zoo (FOTZ)
Garden Center Association
Girl Scouts of America
Gladstone Democratic Club
Greater Kansas City Chamber of Commerce
Heart of America Labor Council
Hispanic Chamber of Commerce
Historical Society of New Santa Fe
Howard, Needles, Tammen & Bergendoff
International Brotherhood of Electrical Workers
Junior League of Kansas City, Missouri
Kansas City Northern Miniature Railroad Association
Kansas City Power and Light
Kansas City Rose Society

Kansas City Young Matrons
Kansas City Zoo Docents
Kessler Society
Lakeside Nature Center Volunteers
Liberty Memorial Association
Metro Medical Society of Greater Kansas City
Metropolitan Kansas City Board of Realtors
Mill Creek Park Association
Missouri Restaurant Association
Missouri State Conservation Commission
Motel & Hotel Association of Greater Kansas City, Inc.
National Association of Women in Construction
Native Sons of Kansas City
Nickerson Irrigation
Northland Betterment Committee
Northland Committee for the New Zoo
Northland Chamber of Commerce
Partners in Swope Park
Penn Valley Park Fitness Trail Association
Penn Valley Park Neighborhood Association
Platte County Business-Professional Association
Prairie Gateway Chapter, ASLA
Retired Seniors Volunteer Program (RSVP)
Shoal Creek Association
Silver Haired Council
South Kansas City Chamber of Commerce
Southwestern Bell Pioneers
Starlight Theatre Association
Thomas Hart Benton Group/Sierra Club
Townsend Communications
Tuttle-Ayers-Woodward
Unico National
Union Cemetery Historical Society
Volunteers in Parks Program (VIP)
Westport Garden Club
Westport Historical Society
Whole Person, Inc.
Wild Berry Neighborhood Association

ACKNOWLEDGEMENTS

This book is the result of a cooperative effort by members of the board and staff of Parks and Recreation; civic leaders and city officials; and writers, historians, designers and photographers.

We would especially like to thank Mrs. Gerald W. Gorman, president of the park board during the time this book was being produced, and the two other commissioners, Ollie W. Gates and Carl J. DiCapo; Terry R. Dopson, park director; Mark L. McHenry, deputy director; Michael R. Herron, manager of boulevard services and secretary to the park board; Victoria Liston Roque, manager of administrative services; Jerry D. John, manager of construction services; George L. Eib, manager of horticultural services; Stephen F. Lampone, manager of park services; Michael H. Malyn, manager of planning services; Mary Edith Lillis, superintendent of recreation; Johnny Ford, manager of specialized services; James Shoemaker, park planner; and Ralph Waterhouse, former director of the zoo. Other park staff members who helped gather material and answer innumerable questions were: James O'Shea, landscape architect; Charles Isaacson; public relations specialist; William Cavole, graphic specialist; Al Safady, accountant; and Dorothy Shelby, secretary.

Former park commissioners who provided valuable insights were Jerome Cohen, Davis Jackson, Richard Marr, Lewis Dysart, Dr. Robert Hodge, and L. P. Cookingham. Willis Theis, son of former commissioner Frank Theis, and Frank Theis, grandson; and Frank Sebree, grandson of former commissioner Frank Sebree, recalled for us significant past events.

Former park personnel who were interviewed included Frank Vaydik and Jerry Darter, former park directors; and Richard E. Soper, former board secretary. John Ayres gave valuable information about his father. W. I. Ayers, longtime park draftsman and engineer. Gordon Whiffen, former landscape architect with Hare & Hare, offered information about the designing of some parks in the system.

Our appreciation is extended also to numerous city officials including David Olson, city manager; Richard Berkley, Ilus Davis, and Charles Wheeler, former mayors; and Robert Kipp, former city manager, for the time they gave to being interviewed.

Civic leaders who offered important information through interviews included: Jonathan Kemper, president, Commerce Bank; Donald Hall, chairman of the board, Hallmark Cards Inc.; Miller Nichols, chairman of the board, J. C. Nichols Company, and Albert Mauro, vice-president of Kansas City Southern Industries and president of the Friends of the Zoo. Susan Perry, Mrs. Clyde Nichols, Mrs. Frank Werner, Arlene Payne, and Mrs. Moulton Green, who work with the park board on a voluntary basis, also gave valuable assistance.

Lucile Bluford, editor of the *Kansas City Call*, and Atwell L. (Al) Bohling, former editorial writer of the *Kansas City Star*, contributed important insights into park board activities.

In addition, we would like to thank a number of historians: Martha R. Clevenger, associate archivist, Missouri Historical Society; William H. Wilson, professor of history, University of North Texas; Dave Boutross, associate director, Western Missouri Historical Manuscripts; George Ehrlich, professor of art and art history and Lawrence Larsen, professor of history at the University of Missouri-Kansas City; Kurt Culbertson, Aspen, Colorado, landscape architect; Roger Werner, former president of Historic Merriam, Inc.; and the staff of the Missouri Valley Room of the Kansas City Public Library.

Credit for the research, writing and designing of the book goes to Jane Mobley who headed the project; art director Vivian Strand; writer/researcher Nancy Harris; interviewer Andrea Whitmore; proofreader Beth Scalet; intern Molly Maxwell and administrative assistant Licia Clifton-James.

The black and white plans used for the hand-colored division pages are courtesy of Ochsner Hare & Hare for pages 26-27, Loose Park, pages 42-43, the Nelson-Atkins Museum of Art and the front and back end pages of Ward Parkway; and Kansas City Parks and Recreation for pages xii-1, The Paseo and pages 58-59, Swope Park. The plans were hand-colored by Vivian Strand. The color plan on pages 78-79 is courtesy of the American Society of Landscape Architects, Prairie Gateway Chapter.

Photo Credits: Steven Ginn: viii, Music Pavilion; 2, Swope Park Gate; 44, J.C. Nichols Fountain; 48, Starlight Theatre; 50, Spirit of Freedom Fountain; 56, Meyer Circle Fountain; 62, Walk on the Grass sign; 66, trees on Blue River; 70, man fishing; 70, Swope Park Golf Course; 72, tennis courts; 82, tulips sleeping sign; 84, sunset on Brush Creek; 86, Moore Sculpture Garden; 92, sunset at Swope Park. Roy Inman: 52, J.C. Nichols Fountain. Vivian Strand: 77, bicyclists. Frank Theis: 28, Loose Park Lake; 60, Solar Field. Stephen Thornton: 94, Anita Gorman and Ollie Gates. Carol Vanderwal of Hallmark Cards, Inc.: 34, Loose Park Rose Garden. All other photographs are courtesy of Kansas City Parks and Recreation.

A CITY WITHIN A PARK
One Hundred Years of Parks and Boulevards
in Kansas City, Missouri

was created by Highwater Editions, digitally composed in Minion
and printed on Warren's Lustro Offset Enamel Gloss,
a neutral pII paper with an expected 300-year
library-storage life as determined by the
Council of Library Resources of the
American Library Association

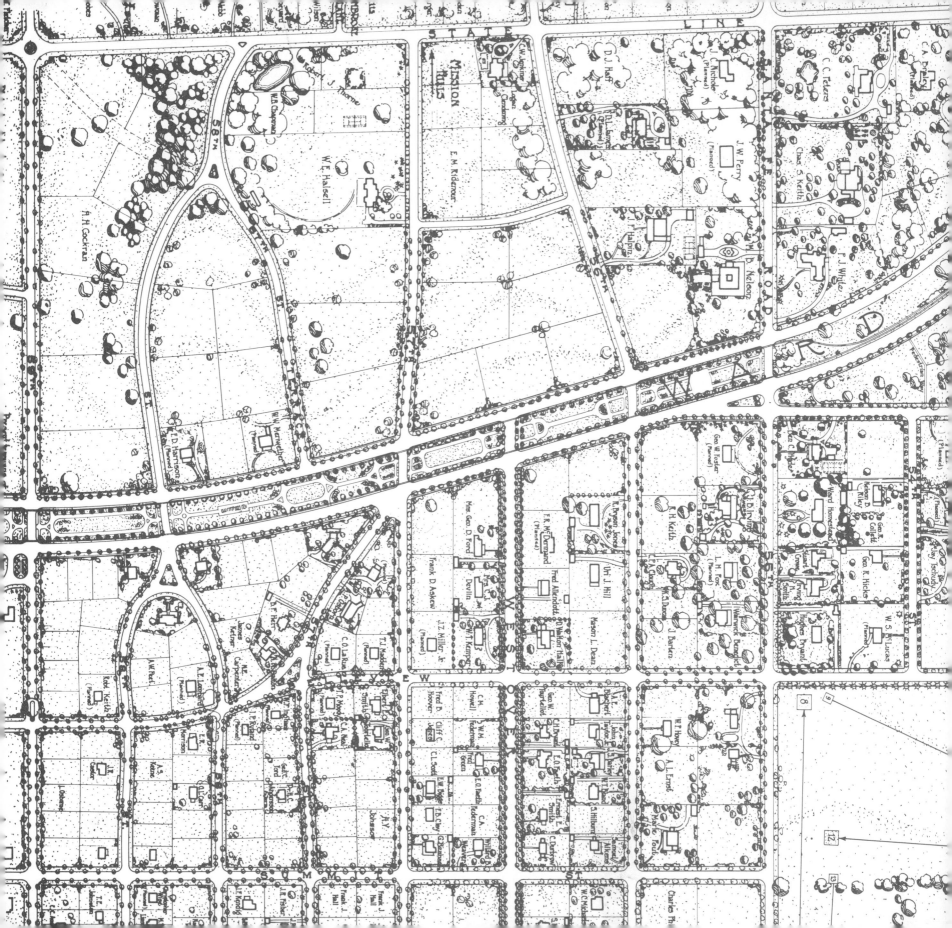